IN THE
OF THE GODS

CULT INK

IN THE LAP OF THE GODS
A QUEEN AND FREDDIE MERCURY ANTHOLOGY

EDITED BY
DAVID GELDARD
and
JAY GENT

'IN THE LAP OF THE GODS: A QUEEN AND FREDDIE MERCURY ANTHOLOGY'

A Cult Ink Books Publication

Editors: David Geldard and Jay Gent

ISBN: 9798312430585

First Edition © 2025 Cult Ink Books

All essays are copyright their respective authors

Front and back cover illustration © Jim Sangster

Logo design, layout and typesetting by Jay Gent

Additional editing & proofing by Russ J. Graham

Typeset in Palatino Linotype Version 1.40

All royalties from this volume will be donated to

The Mercury Phoenix Trust

https://www.mercuryphoenixtrust.org/

Please respect the charity by not sharing material from this volume over the internet

Contents

Good Company	Peter Straker	7
Where It All Began	Shirley Dyson	11
News Of The World, Read All About It..	Alan G. Parker	15
A Complex, Sudden, Strange and Deep Love	Michele Kurlander	26
Ray Burdis: Producing the Freddie Mercury Tribute Concert	David Geldard	31
Better Things: Clayton Moss Interview	David Geldard	37
In The Land That Our Grandchildren Knew...	Sam R.M. Geden	40
Those Were The Days Of My Life	Carl Potter	53
Queen - A Covers Band	Richard Hearn	62
Hope And Glory: My Life Through Queen	Fiona Nicholas	69
Aura(l) Pleasures – Queen's 'Flash Gordon' Soundtrack	Don Klees	72
Peter Freestone Interview	David Geldard	76
Live Killers	Jim Jenkins	88
Over The Rainbow	Martin Green	107
Missed Opportunities	Teo Torriatte	111
Denise Silcock Interview	David Geldard	115
Celluloid Heroes (With Just A Twist Of VT)	Ken Shinn	125
The Spare Ticket	Mick Hoole	142

How Queen Helped Me Survive Adolescence	Fotini Drakou	145
Jeff Scott Soto Interview	David Geldard	148
Queen Always Kept Me In A 'Drowse'	Sue Duris	155
Gettin' Smile: Track by Track	Tim Staffell	160
Front Page News: Discovering (And Rediscovering) Queen	Georg Purvis	165
I Never Saw Queen Live	Gary Rockwell	170
Doin' Alright: The Doug Bogie Interview	David Geldard	174
Admiring Queen... From The Other Side Of The World	Chris Lee	188
In the Lap of the Pods Interview	David Geldard	192
Growing Up With Queen	Kari van ter Beek	202
Man From Manhattan: The Eddie Howell Interview	David Geldard	206
Dear Friends	Jon Fowler	220
Queen Fans - The New Generation	Hannah Dennis	231
Friends Will Be Friends Will Be Friends	Paul Webb	233
As It Began: Jim Jenkins Interview	David Geldard	238
Funny How Love Is	David Geldard	248
Very Special Thanks		276

Good Company

Peter Straker remembers Freddie Mercury

Peter & Freddie [Photo © Wendy Allison/Cherry Red Records)

'Hair' was THE first internationally acclaimed rock musical, so I suppose that's where it started... I was lucky because when I did 'Hair', I was signed to Polydor and did some singles with them. It was a wonderful experience. So that's how I got into that area of rock. Then I met up with John Reid and Elton John. I went to see Elton do a couple of big concerts and that was quite magical for me, even after doing 'Hair'. It just went from there and then subsequently through David Minns [one of Freddie's first male partners] and John Reid, I met Freddie Mercury.

When I met Freddie, after about seven or eight months I asked him if he would produce an album for me ['This One's On Me', 1977] and he said yes! I was very lucky because John Reid brokered the deal with EMI and Rocket Records and so I was able to make these three albums.

Working with Freddie on the album was fantastic. Looking back, it was great. I had no experience of recording, I mean, I'd done singles and things like that but this was quite intense and quite good because I learned a hell of a lot. Freddie asked me, "Would you mind if I asked Roy Thomas Baker to help with it?" because, of course, Queen were working with him. I said, "Of course! Why not?". You either like that music or you don't and I happen to love what Queen do, so it wasn't very difficult for me.

I really like 'Heart Be Still'. Also, 'Ragtime Piano Joe', that was just wonderful because I had a big hit in Europe. I think it went quite high up in the charts in Holland, it was there for weeks. It did well in Germany too, and in Belgium and Luxembourg. It did very, very well for me and it was written by two of my friends, Annabel Levington (who I was in 'Hair' with), and Don Fraser (who was my musical director at the time).

That was really fun because I was doing that in my show at the time. Freddie and Queen came to that show, which included a lot of those songs which are on that first album.

Peter & Freddie in the studio
[Photo © Wendy Allison/Cherry Red Records)

I really did enjoy working musically with him and I'm not just saying that, because I learned a hell of a lot at the time. He suggested to me to write songs because it never occurred to me to write songs. I became more and more interested in the idea and I did write a few songs. All the songs that I'd sung previously were all other people's songs and I'd just interpreted them. That was quite fantastic.

Freddie had a lot to do with the other two albums ['Changeling', 1979; 'Real Natural Man', 1980] although he wasn't the producer – looking back he was almost like a mentor. He used to come in and do some backing singing with me and the band. So, he was quite hands on with all three albums really. He was my friend and he was very helpful.

That was one of the great things, but on the other side his generosity of spirit and his great desire for having fun. We loved the theatre; we loved the same stuff in the theatre. We loved the ballet and opera. We just got on very, very well. There were lots of things, it was great fun! We drank a lot; we had a good time and we had a laugh. He was good company, very funny, very witty, and we used to send each other up terribly with great humour, not with any nastiness. I had fantastic times with Freddie and with the band when we all went out; they were a very generous group of people I have to say.

I had a great time doing [Freddie Mercury & Montserrat Caballe album] 'Barcelona' because a lot of my friends were on it, like Carol Woods. She was the lead singer in a show I was doing in the West End at the time called 'Blues In The Night', and Freddie came to see that show so many times.

'Barcelona' was great, great fun. I was lucky enough to hear some of the melodies, probably before other people and when he and Mike Moran were working on it, it was quite exciting. Also, quite daunting, I have to say, because I thought 'how is this going to work?' But they made it work, as history as shown us. It was a fantastic idea that Freddie came up with, quite unique for that time. It was inspired and it stands on its own. Brilliant.

Peter Straker was speaking to David Geldard.

*Originally published in **We Are Cult**, 1 April 2020.*

Where It All Began

Memories Of Queen Over The Decades

Shirley Dyson

On reflection, the magic of Queen began for me on 18 September 1976 – the picnic in the park, Queen's free concert in Hyde Park.

It was the 'A Night at the Opera' album that had first drawn me in, the music and the unique harmonies of Queen were like nothing else I had ever heard before, plus the combination of live theatre, the costumes and drama, but most of all the music, so beautifully reproduced live on stage. It was something I had not experienced before.

Back to that September day, it was a beautiful one, a perfect summer's day, deep blue skies and a light breeze. It was an early start and with a friend I made it to Hyde Park in plenty of time to claim a spot on the grass very near the stage, right in the centre. Queen weren't due to appear until about 7.30 or so, but there were other acts to keep us entertained including the lovely Kiki Dee, standing next to a life-size cardboard cut-out of Elton John.

Before the entertainment started, we were quite happy watching the whole set up by the roadies and sound engineers accompanied by the amazing tracks from Pink Floyd's latest album and 'Shine on you Crazy Diamond' wafting through the entire Park. The afternoon turned slowly into dusk and when the moment arrived the excitement grew, bright lights lit up the stage and clouds of dry ice drifted into the crowd.

Brian, John and Roger were in their places, soon to be joined by Freddie, who burst onto the stage, a vision in a white leotard, his mane of glossy black hair falling around his shoulders, a tinge of blusher on his high cheekbones and kohl eyeliner around those beautiful dark eyes. No-one could match that unique voice, those moves or his stage presence! Brian, Roger and John all added their own magic.

It was a live show like no other, the music and harmonies perfectly reproduced and the costume changes a real feast for the eyes. This was my first Queen concert and I was eager for more when it was all over, to the strains of God Save the Queen.

On our way out of the park, the first of many friendships were started and the circle grew as we became Fan Club members, started to buy all the Queen merchandise on offer and Freddie fans painting our finger-nails on our left hands black when going to all the concerts. It was fun dressing up. Queen were certainly responsible for bringing out the creativity in us, we painted portraits (usually of Freddie), composed poems and Brian fans making penguins of all sizes because he liked them!

How lucky we were in the '70s to get close to our heroes, and get their autographs on so many occasions – no 'selfies' then. We would repeat these wonderful experiences time and time again. Freddie, we soon discovered, was quite shy and softly spoken but also had a delightful sense of humour. Once, on being asked if he could be kissed, he replied, "Oh, you have to pay for those my dear."

Several concerts followed, particularly at Wembley, and, in the early days, before the curtain went up we would usually be listening to the music of Chopin, Freddie's favourite composer. This would be followed by clouds of dry ice drifting out from under the curtain as the excitement grew and once again we were witnessing a show like no other.

There were often opportunities to see them, whether it was at a venue or an airport, and occasionally backstage out to where their limousines were parked. It was Brian who usually obliged with a chat, an autograph and one time I managed to give him a kiss. My 10-year-old son was with me and later told his grandma he was not amused and very embarrassed. However, he loved the show and used to do a fair imitation of Freddie!

In October 1977, our little circle of friends got an invitation as members of the Fan Club to appear in the making of the video for 'We Are The Champions'. While waiting to be called into the theatre, we were filmed along the pavement outside singing 'Killer Queen', not realising that decades later, this little segment would be shown in a documentary called 'Days of our Lives'. To see oneself in close-up on the TV screen decades later was very unexpected and something of a shock, to say the least!

The last concert I was lucky enough to see was the Freddie Mercury Tribute Concert at Wembley which was an unforgettable experience, albeit a very sad one. All the artistes involved, and they were numerous, gave their all – Freddie would have been proud. George Michael in particular, his voice so similar to Freddie's, on that day singing 'Somebody to Love'.

At the very end we were treated to a magnificent firework display which was the perfect ending to such a memorable and exciting tribute to the greatest showman ever. Freddie followed his dream, what an inspiration he was, and left us the precious gift of his amazing legacy.

Later, with the arrival of Facebook, many of us who had lost touch for a while, got together again, now with ages ranging from 65 to 80, still recalling the amazing times we had during those years and feeling so blessed to have been a part of those very special times, never to be forgotten.

News Of The World, Read All About It...

Alan G. Parker

"My new purple shoes, Bin amazin' the people next door and my rock'n'roll forty fives. Bin enragin' the folks on the lower floor. I got a way with the girls on my block, try my best to be a real individual. And when we go down to smokies and rock, they line up like it's some kind of ritual"

– 'Tenement Funster'

I was a child of the seventies, with, very much thanks to my parents, a bedroom covered in pop posters, and a few T-Shirts to match, because Dad was a big music fan (a dedicated jazz man) it was very much encouraged.

I don't remember a time when both me and my brother didn't have a stack of singles, and via birthdays and Christmas a few albums too. 'Top Of The Pops' on BBC 1 Thursday night was more like our church than simply a TV show. The bands we presumed must have been beamed in from Mars, because guys like these surely didn't live on the same planet that we called home! Our heroes included Slade, Sweet, The Glitter Band, and the tartan terrors as my Mum referred to them; you might know them better as the Bay City Rollers. If there had been a Mastermind round specifically on the Rollers in 1975 when I was 10 years old, I'd have walked it, but I digress.

In addition to all the aforementioned, two more artists were sneaking into my world, and taking up more space (that we didn't have) on the bedroom wall (thank God Dad was a painter and decorator, he started putting posters on the bedroom ceiling for us!). One of them came out of a family holiday to Blackpool, where I discovered Elton John, or 'Captain Fantastic' as I thought he was called for the longest time. And the others were a bunch of skinny individuals who wore silk and black nail polish, they answered to the collective name Queen. "Good set of pipes on him that lad," said my Dad, before going back to his newspaper; "They are gonna go places, you mark my words if they don't."

At this point it might be worth adding some background, because without it you might not make too much sense of where this is ultimately going. I was born in April 1965, with a condition known as macrocephaly, not helped much by the fact that I was a little skinny thing, a bit of a church mouse figure, you'd rarely see me shouting boo near a goose! At junior school I was very badly bullied, so while the other kids were out playing at nights and weekends, I was in my bedroom creating a world of my own, Marvel Comics, 'Doctor Who', the 'Planet of the Apes' TV series, 'Starsky & Hutch' and these pop stars who helped create my safety net. I don't really remember playing out much until I went to secondary school and got a newspaper round, all the other kids who did newspaper rounds were older than me, so they told me to come out more, they would look after the bullies, they thought I was cool because I had a good record collection and a knowledge of music way beyond my years. Mark Jones owned 'Queen II', he was three years my senior (a lifetime at that age) and at weekends sometimes wore eyeliner! Mark was cool, and I needed that in my life.

Given my personal history of books, CDs and movies that I've been involved in over the years, there might be a lot of people reading this thinking that I spent much of the summer of 1977 waiting patiently for the release of 'Never Mind The Bollocks', the debut album from the Sex Pistols. But that couldn't be further from the truth. Aged 12 I had no idea who the Sex Pistols were. The album I was waiting not so patiently for all year was, it later turned out, released on the same day as 'NMTB', 28 October 1977, and had been recorded at Wessex Studios in London between July and September, next door to the studio where the Pistols were working. There was a famous and much told story regarding a chance meeting at the studio between Freddie Mercury and Sid Vicious, or 'Simon Ferocious' as Fred had christened him! "Ah, Freddie," sneered Sid, "have you succeeded in bringing ballet to the masses yet?" (a reference to an interview Mercury had recently done with the UK music press) "We're doing our best, dear," replied Fred. Queen later admitted that they thought the Pistols were alright, but that Sid was a bit of a buffoon.

By early 1977 I personally owned three Queen albums ('Sheer Heart Attack', 'A Night at the Opera' and 'A Day at the Races') and a dozen singles. More importantly for an impressionable 11-year-old, going on 12, there were two Queen badges on my denim jacket, you remember the ones – they were bigger than Captain America's shield – and I had a Queen patch sewn onto the back courtesy of my Gran. The group were also hogging some of that precious bedroom wall space, and in Blackpool that year I got my first Queen T-Shirt. Something was about to happen that year that hadn't happened before, or at least since I'd discovered Queen: They were going to release a new album. One that I'd be able to buy on release day. Proceedings began on 7 October with the release of a new single 'We Are The Champions'/'We Will Rock You', which I bought on release day from AMES in Blackburn. It was a masterpiece, and I played both sides of the single constantly. Dad said that the real strength of any single was that you could get enjoyment out of both sides, if the B-side was naff, it didn't bode well for the album.

> "I feel the Queen style of well-produced or production sort of albums is over. We've done to death multi-tracked harmonies and, for our own sakes and for the public's, we want to go on to a different sort of project. And the next album will be that." - Freddie Mercury

Exactly eleven days later on 28 October I went into town with Dad to get 'News Of The World'. My overriding memory of that Saturday is that all the record shops in Blackburn, Lancashire (my home town), were green, or seemed to be green! Even the record departments of big stores, all green with occasional silver plastic robots, holding albums. 'News Of The World' wasn't only upon us, it was big, the kind of big that leaves a lasting impression. We got the album (again from AMES), bought a 'NOTW' badge, which instantly found a place in my denim jacket (I've still got it to this day), and then got the bus home. I looked at every inch of the sleeve, it was mesmerising, a giant robot either attacking or saving Queen on a background that looked like mass hysteria! In later years I found out that the robot, now affectionately known as 'Frank', had originally been drawn by Frank Kelly Freas in 1953 for the cover of sci-fi magazine 'Astounding

Science Fiction' (October 1953 issue), under the original sub-title of "Please, fix it... Daddy?"

While at university, it seems a young Roger Taylor owned a copy of this magazine. When he presented the group with the magazine in 1977 saying it would make a great album cover, especially if the wounded solider which the robot was originally holding was replaced by the band members themselves, the initial reaction from his band mates was the worry that Frank Kelly Freas may no longer still be with us. When it turned out he was alive and well in the USA, a plan began to fall into place for an album that might have been called 'Duck Soup', following the previous albums Marx Brothers theme. But was now ready to take a very different path.

For his part, Frank Kelly Freas was a classical music fan, and didn't have a clue who Queen were. One of the reasons the audience is fleeing scared from the auditorium on the album's gatefold while the robot looks on, is best summed up in his own words: "Because I thought I might just hate them, and it would ruin my ideas." In the end of course he became a huge fan. For my part, when we arrived home on that Saturday in October 1977 my copy of 'News Of The World' hit the turntable while I sat with a can of Coke looking at the sleeve. The album kicked off with 'We Will Rock You' (Brian said he wanted the song to be simple) followed by 'We Are The Champions' (which Freddie later claimed he wrote in 1975). Both were familiar to me, and riding high in the UK singles charts both were stomping stadium rockers, and thus incredibly brave at the height of punk. These songs simply wouldn't work in a sweaty London club, they begged to be played in stadiums with audiences of 80,000+. And indeed they would be before the year was out. Track three was 'Sheer Heart Attack', a song Roger had been toying with since 1974...

> "By the time I had finished the song, we were two albums later, so it just struggled out on the 'News Of The World' album. It's quite interesting, because we were making an album next door to a punk band, the Sex Pistols, and it really fit into that punk explosion that was happening at the time. It was actually better that it happened that it came out on the 'News Of The World' album." - Roger Taylor, about 'Sheer Heart Attack'

Side one continued with a ballad written by Brian May inspired by the death of his pet cat, and titled 'All Dead, All Dead'. It would quite honestly melt the hardest of hearts. That in turn was followed by 'Spread Your Wings', a song by John Deacon and quite possibly my favourite Queen song of all time. It became the second single from the album, but with Queen away touring the USA it vanished without trace peaking at number 34 in the UK charts, despite a brilliant promo video shot in Roger's back garden. It was the first Queen single ever to contain no backing vocals. 'Fight From The Inside' ended side one. Virtually a solo song from Roger, it was hard, to some degree aggressive, and suited the current musical climate. Slash from Guns N' Roses would later say it was one of his favourite guitar riffs of all time.

Even at the tender age of 12 it was easy to see that this album was going to have a lasting effect on me. The first side had blown me away. Side two opened with 'Get Down, Make Love' possibly the most sexual song in the whole Queen catalogue. I remember Mum walking through the room and looking across as if to say "What on earth is this you're listening to?" 'Sleeping on the Sidewalk', quite possibly the closest Queen ever got to singing the blues, was up next, and I remember that it was the only song on the album that I had to listen to more than once to fully appreciate. 'Who Needs You' follows, another one from John Deacon. It was years later through good studio headphones that I learnt Freddie's vocal is completely on the right-hand side!

A Brian May number titled 'It's Late' follows. Brian would later say that it was the very first time he'd ever written a song by treating it like a three-act theatrical play. A Freddie song, 'My Melancholy Blues', closes the album. The song contains no backing vocals or guitars, rather odd for Queen track, but there you go. As I put the album back into its sleeve, I remember thinking that side two wasn't as strong as side one, but that it was a grower. In October 1977 my favourite Queen album was 'Sheer Heart Attack' but that was all about to change.

One night in early December 1977, Dad came home from work with a huge cardboard cut-out of the robot holding Queen on a green background. He had been painting the bakery next door to one of the town's record stores when he saw someone taking the big cardboard display to the bin. He told them his son would love that, to which they replied, "Cool, it's yours!" It began a trend regarding the robot and the album and me. On a summer holiday to Spain in 1978 Grandma and Grandad found another T-Shirt with the robot on it, so they brought me one back, while a trip to Preston with Mum resulted in more 'NOTW' badges from a market stall. Despite the punk rock backdrop to which it was released, 'News of the World' reached number 3 in the UK and a very healthy number 4 in the USA, a market the group were still working on completely cracking. A third single, 'It's Late', was released in 1978 but only in the USA, Canada, Japan and New Zealand.

Following the tour to support 'A Day At The Races' in 1976, the group had re-entered the studio in July 1977. According to most reports in the music press of the time they were very much set on an album to be named 'Duck Soup', continuing their Marx Brothers trend. But with an eye on the changing trends in both music and fashion, thanks to Roger Taylor, they had already decided that the new album would have a much more basic feel to it; not everything needed to be layered or indeed multi-layered, indeed the plan was to make an album that could easily be recreated on a live stage, and not to spend forever recording it. They enlisted former collaborator Mike Stone as assistant producer, and set about recording a number of songs that for once weren't heavily dominated by Freddie and Brian. The whole session had an open house feel to it, hence the occasional stray Sex Pistol wandering in from next door! As Freddie later admitted, "I said, 'darlings, it's time to be mainstream'."

> "We'd already made a decision that... [after] 'A Night at the Opera' and 'A Day at the Races', we wanted to go back to basics for 'News of the World'. But it was very timely because the world was looking at punk and things being very stripped down. So, in a sense we were conscious, but it was part of our evolution anyway." – Brian May

The album was completed and mixed in just three months, which for Queen was practically light speed, although they did decamp from Wessex Studio to Sarm West Studios for the final mix. Reports on why they left Wessex vary over the years, but it's likely that they just needed a change of scene and a fresh headspace. Although they had already proved themselves as a killer live band, there was something about 'News Of The World' that almost screamed 'stadium rock band'. It was in many ways the start of the big push, which manager John Reid had been masterminding since they joined him in 1975. The concert tour to support the album began on 11 November 1977 in Portland, USA, and included 21 gigs in Europe. The tour ended on 13 May 1978 in London. It was one of Queen's most successful outings, and as can clearly be seen from bootleg footage of the Earl's Court show, the group are on fire.

The press reception for the album was mixed. Some critics understood what Queen were doing, others simply accused them of bandwagon jumping. The group's faithful army of fans gave it a huge vote of 100% confidence. Indeed, the official fan club membership increased in 1977, and for my part it's the year I joined.

My continued fascination with the album really began to grow once I left school and had access to spare cash. Not unlike The Beatles 'Sgt. Peppers Lonely Hearts Club Band', Elton's 'Captain Fantastic' or Pink Floyd's 'Wish You Were Here', I won't be happy until I own every different copy of 'News Of The World' that I can find. Did you know that in Argentina the album is called 'Noticias Del Mundo'? I do, because there's a framed copy of that version looking straight at me now on the lounge wall. In 1995, during an afternoon stroll, I found myself in Cecil Court, a small alleyway consisting largely of collectors' book shops in London's West End. There I found not one but two copies of the original October 1953 magazine 'Astounding Science Fiction'. I bought them on the spot. I've since had the good fortune to find various trinkets connected to the album across the globe. These include tour programmes, press kits, promotional photographs, green vinyl versions, picture discs, the list goes on and on. My prized possession was acquired here in London, at Sotheby's auctioneers in Kensington during the summer of 2000, when I bought a fully signed copy of the album.

Over the years 'News Of The World' has become a classic, to be name-checked when the long lists are rolled out by the various rock magazines. To me, just seeing 'Frank' the robot represents safety, the transformation of the bullied church-mouse kid into the man he ultimately became, or at least the start of that road.

In 2017, the group released a 40th Anniversary box set edition of the album that contained everything including the kitchen sink, plus a brilliant documentary with footage from both the studio and the world tour, along with a bonus CD of alternative takes from the studio titled 'Raw Sessions'.

The album and the robot have appeared in the US animated comedy 'Family Guy', and became part of Marvel Comics X-Men universe via an incredibly limited-edition album and comic book. The cover, by artist Mike Del Mindo, depicts a Sentinel holding Old Man Logan and Kitty Pryde as Colossus plummets to the ground. Don't expect much change out of £1,000 for a copy of that particular version. One day maybe I'll own one of the original in-store plastic robots from 1977.

Film director Alan G. Parker with Brian May, September 2011.
[Photo © A. G. Parker]

During the Queen + Adam Lambert tour of 2017, an animated 'Frank' now features heavily in the show, and it was this version of the robot that graced the cover of the Record Store Day 12" version of 'We Are the Champions'/'We Will Rock You' – a record I was queueing for at 6am outside Sister Ray Records in London on the day!

Obsessed is a funny word, but I fully admit I'm completely that way about 'News of the World'. When I interviewed Brian May in September 2011, I asked him to sign my 2 CD set. "Is this your favourite Queen album?" he asked me, and my reply was simple: "It's a part of my fabric, Brian, from being 12 years old". He gave me a hug, the world continued to turn and somewhere in the universe I know that 'Frank' smiled...

A Complex, Sudden, Strange and Deep Love

Michele Kurlander

'Somebody To Love' is not always my favorite song. How can I choose just one? Queen and Freddie are complex and apt to reinvent their music periodically, while so good at fulfilling their promise within the confines of any such reinvention, that falling in love with Queen or Freddie or both requires an understanding that there is always something to adore, whatever my mood or circumstance.

Some days I want to sink into the arms of my stuffed chair, close my eyes, and sigh while I let Freddie 'Take my Breath Away' through giant earphones.

Sometimes, a funky me needs a bare-chested Freddie in tight white pants as he slinks and provocatively struts , fist bumps and pirouettes swiftly around the sounds of 'Dragon Attack' – while Brian's face is in deep concentration as his guitar excites and squeals and Roger bites his lip and grimaces as his arms, with impossible speed, womp and clatter and attack his kit, and quiet John maintains a passive expression, and a childlike bounce as he causes my innards to clench at the insistent bass beat.

Then sometimes I have to watch at Wembley, enraptured when Freddie first credits Brian with the writing, and, as Brian plays his electric piano with a small smile Freddie sadly, and emotionally expresses why he doesn't 'want to live forever'. He starts out thoughtfully, his lips against the mic, and at one point is so passionate that he stands on tiptoe as he throws his head back and cries the lyrics to the sky.

Or I lean close to my PC screen, elbows on my computer table while a long haired, tight black suited apparition leans back and cries out to me and the heavens that I am a 'Liar!' – and the camera scrolls to those long fingers insistently plucking that bass.

How did it begin? I wandered into a nearby theater in 2018 to watch a so-called "biopic" that I have now come to despise much of. I learned that day about a group of musicians I knew little about.

I was intrigued by the creation on a farm of a track consisting of a joining of tenuously related sounds and genres that I had heard before but never before paid much attention to.

I had also not previously heard of Live Aid but there it was and – wow! At the end of the credits, a tall young man with animal magnetism and an amazing voice told me how he couldn't be stopped. I left the theater singing 'Don't Stop Me Now' at the top of my lungs.

Someone told me that the record company exec was really Mike Myers. Really? So I went back to see.

And then back again – seven times in all.

I was a bit annoyed at the childish selfishness of the main character, but forgave him because of the music he created.

It was after that, on an airplane to France on New Year's Eve, that I saw a documentary about the making of 'Night At the Opera' and learned about his genius, and Brian's banjolele, and became fascinated by the anger in 'Death On Two Legs' and discovered that the album was much more than 'Bo Rhap' and Freddie, much more than what I saw in the movie.

And now almost three years later, I am a constantly contributing member in three Queen groups, a lover of all of the concerts that are reachable online, a lover of dancing and Queen music joined by the Bejart Ballet, and a rapt watcher of all of the interviews.

And I have fallen impossibly in love. How could I not? Although the love of my life is rumored to have died in 1991, that is simply not possible. He laughs and flirts with interviewers on my TV or PC screen and sometimes gazes out at me with those deep brown eyes.

He scowls and smiles and relates to people, and causes his voice to soar or growl or sooth at will onstage or in videos, as I can see through the miracle of YouTube.

He still sings and plays piano and gives out presents to all who he loves through the memories of Mike Moran and Peter Freestone and Peter Straker and Rheinhold Mack and Rudi Dolezal and all those whose lives he actually touched.

And there are the true stories!

There is the employee, whose mother died just before his birthday, who received a call at his home. "Hi – just call me 'mother' and get into the car at your curb," and was whisked away to

Garden Lodge for a birthday party.

There is the dancer who fell and concussed during the 'I Was Born To Love You' video and was taken to the hospital by ambulance, accompanied by a bare-chested handsome man in tight white pants who remained at the hospital until she was pronounced safe, who only then returned to the video shoot at 2 a.m.

There are all of the unattributed monies distributed to families who lost jobs or loved ones and whose plight came to his ear.

There is the day when his throat was bloodied by the effort to complete recording John's 'Another One Bites the Dust' so it was perfect, despite the others being less than enamoured by that track.

It didn't take long for me to discover that Rami was playing a man who looked a bit like Freddie and sang and performed like Freddie but was devoid of the loyalty, love, humour, beauty of spirit and discipline of the real Freddie I had come to love so deeply – who never would have left his friends – and never did, but exhausted himself on tour with them when during the movie plot timeline he was supposedly hiding from them.

So I stopped watching. But as it has done with so many others, it got me here. As an aside, I do find myself sending people copies of the May 1985 Tokyo gig to prove he wasn't hiding out before Live Aid but at the tail-end of a long and exhausting tour with the others.

My man supports his friends by refusing in interviews to let anyone even hint that he is more important than any of them; he gives aid and comfort to Roger and John as they gain their writing legs; he supports Brian by gifting him a tape of his own solos, or by visiting him in the hospital to reassure him that his illness will not affect his standing in the band; or, in 1991, he helps Brian recognize and own his future role as a soloist.

He talks to interviewers who he trusts (the rare few) with introspection and thought about himself, the others, his life, the industry, and his love of his work, and with humor.

He was – is – a beautiful, talented, gifted, caring, loving, fun, disciplined, exciting friend and performer and because of the gift of modern technology, will always be so and will always seem to be right next to me. It is not possible to meet another like him. But I don't need to, since he is still here – and I adore him.

Ray Burdis: Producing the Freddie Mercury Tribute Concert

Actor, screenwriter, director & producer Ray Burdis produced The Freddie Mercury Tribute Concert for television.

I was there at the 'Freddie Mercury Tribute Concert', quite near the front. It was one of the best days of my life and I have watched it a million times since on VHS, DVD and Blu-ray. I am interested in how you came to be the producer of it?

From the beginning really. Jim Beach, the band's manager was a partner of mine in a film production company, Fugitive. We were responsible for making a lot of pop promos at the time, one of the largest pop promo companies going. We did 'The Krays' movie too, the original.

That was a great film!

So, with Jim being a partner, when the 'Freddie Mercury Tribute Concert' came up, Jim trusted us to produce that for television. So we got the honour of that and we didn't realise it was going to be such a huge event. We knew it would be big but I think it outdone Live Aid, I'm not sure?

I think it did, yes.

So, obviously, it's a long time ago and my memory is very sketchy. The sheer scale of the production was terrifying, for my partner and myself. I had no idea. We'd done film production but film production is more controllable. You're either on a set or a location. This was massive and to work alongside the rock n' roll teams, I think it was Gerry Stickells at the time, coming in with designs for stages and then we had to bring in lighting designers because it had to be lit for the show, but we had to consider our lighting for television. It was a huge, military operation, putting the whole thing together.

I always looked after myself on a shoot. When it came to the car parking situation for all the people involved, both the rock n' roll side and our production, the space was so tight. Every foot was sought after. One of their planners was saying, "Well, you put your truck there, and yours plugs into there...", there were hundreds of bits of kit out the back. He goes, "What's that bloody great big thing?". It was the biggest square box on the plan. What I didn't want to tell him was that it was my winnebago! My argument was, "Look, we have to have artists, if they want to chat to us and come and see us, we can't do it in a box. It's got to be the winnebago". Plus, we've got our staff and somehow, I blagged it and they went, "Alright then".

I think they were a bit pissed off I had the biggest winnebago on site but it did go to use. There was a bit of controversy going on with Elton John and Axl Rose. Axl had supposedly made a derogatory comment about homosexuality [the song 'One in a Million']. Elton was a bit pissed off. So we had to talk around, you know what I mean? In the spirit of the occasion, to be fair to Axl, he shook hands and apologised.

There was lots of shenanigans going on. If you think about it, it was a huge rock n' roll event. I was in awe of it, even though I'd worked with many of the artists before. I invited my wife along and I said, "The best time to come is before the audience arrive, come and watch the rehearsal". It was something else! I remember sitting with all my friends, lots of friends and family from the arts, just sitting on the grass, watching Elton John onstage being very relaxed. Y'know, George Michael, the whole lot of them doing their rehearsal. That was a big memory for me.

I bet it was!

You could actually enjoy the performances because once they were up onstage and the show was on the road, we haven't got time to enjoy it. We had to make sure everything ran smoothly. It is a huge, nerve wracking experience but one I am proud to have put my name to. I haven't watched it in years actually.

Do you think that watching it back would bring back the nerves?

I don't tend to wallow in my own work and that was my work, we filmed it and broadcast it. I move on. I can't watch stuff again and again but I might dig it out one day and have a look.

Did you have to have any conversations with Queen themselves?

We knew Queen anyway, but no. Obviously, it was a sort of sombre time. With things like that, you do sit-in meetings and bands come in and say, "This is what we want", but there was no one-on-one. Bear in mind, if you think about it, they were used to putting on their shows, these huge stars. All I've got to do is make a point of countenance. Make sure there's a director in there, he knows what he's doing and hoping that bloody transmitters and satellites don't break down. It is a job. An exotic job, at the end of the day. People just get on, play their music, we point the cameras, the lighting people do the lights and we all get pissed afterwards!

Was it a good piss up?

Oh, yeah! I ended up staying in the winnebago! [laughs]

Did you have much to do with the other bands on the day?

You do, I mean because you are backstage with them, you're mixing with them, a lot of them we'd worked with before, doing their pop promos. In those days, it was very lucrative to make promos. Budgets were around the £150,000 mark for a three-minute video. When you get to meet the bands on set, you're in an intimate studio situation. With a thing like the tribute concert, there's no way anyone's got time, even the artists. They go out, they do their rehearsal, then they are whisked away and they hide themselves. Everyone wants a piece of them and because of that particular event, there was the world's press there. So, it was almost like a conveyor belt. It was long day for them. They were all really professional. I was amazed at people who you might have thought would be a bit diva-ish, there was no room for that on that day, because it wasn't anyone's show. Everyone was there for a reason. For Freddie. So, it was kind of a different atmosphere, they just got on with it. Unlike Live Aid, where all the bands were trying to outdo each other, which Queen nicked anyway, there was none of that. Everyone was sort of together. It permeated throughout the crews, everyone.

Before you were involved with the Freddie Mercury Tribute Concert, were you a fan of Queen yourself?

I like a lot of different types of music. Obviously, Queen were exceptional but I wouldn't say they were my favourite band by any means. I preferred The Who, to be honest. Over the years, time went on and I was partners with Jim Beach for many years, I grew to respect and see how different their music was to other people's. Funnily enough, knowing I was talking to you today, I went to church this morning and coming back I was thinking of a few old Queen songs and thinking, "Bloody hell, they really were exceptional!".

I think that concert did a lot socially as well, it put the HIV/AIDS issue out there and with all those artists putting their names to it, it made people take a bit more notice than perhaps they otherwise would have done. That must make you feel proud to have been involved in it?

Yeah, I think that's true. It was tremendous for AIDS awareness. At that time, a lot of people around us were dying. It was weird because there was that paranoia about it. We all were a bit paranoid. I remember me and my mates going to weightlifting classes and a guy there died of AIDS. Two of my mates went to the doctors thinking they could get it from the metal bars. We laugh now, thinking how stupid that was but at the time... it was like when the pandemic first broke out here, you know? No one quite knew what was going on. I think that concert did bring people together. It's amazing isn't it, if Freddie had it ten, twenty years ago, he'd probably still be alive today.

Did you work on any other Queen stuff?

Yes. Queen were very loyal. If they worked with someone they liked, they kept them. At the time they were working with two directors that they liked very much, Rudi Dolezal and Hannes Rossacher. So we kind of facilitated them when they came over. At that time we were working with everyone.

Ray Burdis was speaking to David Geldard.

Better Things: Clayton Moss Interview

Singer, songwriter, & recording artist Clayton Moss, guitarist and songwriter with The Cross.

How did you get into music and who were you major musical heroes growing up?

I got into music early on through a passion for the guitar, I and I used to love watching the guitar players on 'Top Of The Pops'. My musical heroes, Carlos Santana, Jimi Hendrix, Eric Clapton, Rolling Stones and that great new band Queen.

How did you join The Cross and get to know Roger?

I answered an anonymous advert in the Melody Maker. If it was a box ad it was definitely worth answering.

Were you a Queen fan before that?

Definitely a Queen fan and Roger's song, 'I'm In Love With My Car', was one of my favourite tracks.

What are your favourite memories of being in the band?

Being picked up by a limo to the airport to rehearse and record in Ibiza for the 'Shove It' album and to just to get to know each other. We stayed at the studios for at least a month. I was hanging out with Ronnie Wood, Steve Strange. We got to see James Brown perform at Pacha, we wrote 'Manipulator' after a night out. We all went back to the Studio with Steve Strange. I came up with that chugging guitar riff and it just sort of happened. We finished it off at a studio in London somewhere. And of course the Marquee Christmas gigs in 1992, where the band were joined by Brian May, Roger Daltrey and Tim Staffell – the first time I played 'I'm In Love with My Car' with Roger Taylor, and of course it was me who suggested we do that song when we were coming up with the set.

How would you describe Roger Taylor?

A gentleman Rock Star.

Freddie famously sang on 'Heaven for Everyone'. Did you get to hang out with Freddie and what was he like?

Yes on a few occasions we did get to hang out with Freddie. Roger took us to Freddie's place for afternoon tea once just to meet up and have a chat. He was relaxed and quite reserved, a nice guy.

You guys had a great catalogue of songs and deserved more of the spotlight. Was it frustrating that The Cross weren't more successful than they were?

Yes, for everybody involved really, including the record company. We had Freddie singing on 'Heaven for Everyone' but we couldn't put it out as The Cross with Freddie's vocal on it.

Which Cross song was your favourite?

'Top Of The World Ma' and 'Final Destination'.

I have a couple of bootlegs of the Marquee Christmas gigs in 1992, where the band were joined by Brian May, Roger Daltrey and Tim Staffell. Was that a lot of fun?

A LOT of fun. That is actually one of the highlights of my career with The Cross. Standing on stage next to Roger Daltrey swinging that microphone past my head!

The Cross did a reunion gig in 2013. How did that come about and was it an enjoyable experience?

It was a one-off twenty-year reunion gig. I think Spike [Edney] instigated that one, and it sounded like a fun idea. It was good to see all the guys again, and the music side of things came together surprisingly quickly. I remember being in the dressing room just before going on stage and Roger says to me, "Clayton, have you met Jeff?". I turn around and Jeff Beck's standing in front of me! So for all of the gig I've got Jeff Beck standing stage left watching us, er… no pressure then! Roger did the same thing to me in Montreux, we were doing a TV show. "Clayton, have you met David?", I turn around and it was David Bowie!

Clayton Moss was speaking to David Geldard.

In The Land That Our Grandchildren Knew...

The Queen connections in my MA dissertation film

Sam R.M. Geden

It's 2am, dead of night, September 2020. It's always 2am. No matter how much I tried to bask in the sun, the daylight quickly dwindled whenever I began work. Perhaps it sensed my madness, and knew I could only work, ghoulishly, in the graveyard shift when the rest of the sane world was deathly silent in sleep. I'm hunched over a laptop which is crying out in agony trying to run Adobe Premiere Pro; freezing every five seconds as I try out different blending effects for the sequence of shots illustrating the crazy, beautiful life and death of the Zodiacal Ouroboros using only footage of paint being stirred. I watch the thirty second sequence… The flow still isn't right; the glitter paint footage comes in too quickly. So I move the footage back by about half a second, which means I have to pre-render the whole sequence again. There goes another five minutes, yet the clock's still stuck on 2am. And my laptop screams and huffs and grunts because it was getting on in years and it wasn't ever designed to cope with software like this. It misses the days when I wasn't a film student. As I notice that the next sequence – NASA landing footage set to a face-melting guitar riff by my pal Kam M-P – has different aspect ratios for every shot and I have to roll the pre-rendering boulder up the hill once again, so do I.

Was it all worth it, I ask myself every single time I move a shot by two frames in the timeline and it is followed by a few minutes of rendering; Premiere Pro threatening to crash and my laptop fan nearly burning a hole through my duvet. What have I done? There's no way I can finish this in the way it needs to be done before the deadline. I'm filled with suffocating dread, like the whole silent night is stuffing itself into my throat. Finally, after an anxious eternity, the pre-render finishes and I watch the whole scene: the beautiful, abstract ecosystem of a galaxy and the cosmic rock of seeing actual astronauts in space, landing on a planet – and into Georges Méliès' breath-taking 'Le Voyage dans la Lune' to complete the surreal splendour. Was it all worth it? Was it ever.

But maybe I'm getting ahead of myself. When I started my Master's degree at the University of Essex in 2019, I had a mission. My undergrad dissertation film got away from me in so many ways: the script over-explained the mystery and under-explained the set-up; a six-day shoot turned into ten days; crew were dropping out left and right while I was rearranging the deck chairs of the Titanic… I wanted to redeem myself with a film that was achievable with the resources I had while still having an edge. It had to be less crazy and more manageable.

Then I listened to ''39' while walking through campus one day and I couldn't shake the gravitation pull of sending my characters to space. I don't think the uni will spring for a cheeky shoot up at the International Space Station…

''39' was written by Brian May and tells the story of a group of astronauts looking for a 'new world' for humanity. After they find and colonise said planet, they return back home, only to find that their year-long voyage equated to a century on Earth due to the time dilation effect outlined in Albert Einstein's theory of Special Relativity. You probably already know that May holds a PhD in astrophysics, and so ''39' comes from a place of tested scientific reality than science-fiction. What makes the song so compelling is that May filters this great space epic through the human experience: it's about the effect Einsteinian physics, in all its unfathomable complexities, has on the everyman who volunteered to do their bit to save the human race. It's about the pain of losing everything – the very concepts of culture and home that you rooted your whole identity into – in the relative blink of an eye. It's the very first Queen song I fell in love with, and it was such a thrill to see Queen + Adam Lambert perform it at my first-ever gig: 14 July 2012 at the Hammersmith Apollo.

Now with all that said, I did not want to adapt ''39' wholesale and 'make a Queen film' that was full of reverence for the band and little else. As I was basically playing in Brian May's toy-box, I wanted to make my own toys with the bits that were there, so it still, perhaps vainly, felt like 'my work.' Honestly, adapting a song like this to the letter – even with the kind of fleshing out you would expect of a film – is essentially asking people to sit through half an hour watching a story that was already perfectly told in three-and-a-half minutes. It really needed to say something a bit different to what the song was saying from the off-set.

I thought about what I liked about the song: the human experience. It tells the moment of realisation that the astronaut's loved ones are lost to them so poignantly… But it finishes on that.

What happened next? No matter how painful that moment of realisation was, they have to live the rest of their lives with that loss 'so heavily weighed' on them. How do you restart your life when everything you've ever known and loved is gone? How do you find a sense of normality again? Can you?

That was my angle. The film takes place a year after their return as they try to settle into a new normal, which I thought was a cool twist to the song's voyage: with so much changing in a relative year to them, the next year of their life is insufferably glacial by comparison. The medium of film would allow us to explore the minutiae and conflict of these characters trying to adjust to a new world and the deeper consequences of their journey.

And so I began developing it. The two 'Pioneers' were Karma Kismet and Henry Burt: while Karma struggles with the loss of her wife and daughter, and her general lack of control in the situation she's trapped in, Henry surrenders himself to the great unfathomable powers of happenstance and makes the most of any opportunity he's been given. Together they cover the spectrum of complicated feelings that ''39' teased in its ending refrain 'for my life / still ahead / pity me:' guilt, resolution, bitterness, optimism and the longing to reconnect with something you fear is forever lost.

When it came to building the uncanny new world Karma and Henry come home to, a slightly more unlikely Queen connection was made. On 24 May 2019, I went to a talk given by May for the fiftieth anniversary of the Apollo 11 moon landing at the Science Museum as a treat for surviving my undergrad. Joining him was Lord Martin Rees, the Astronomer Royal, and the two had a genuinely fascinating talk about the past, present and future of space travel. What stuck out most to me was Rees' belief that the long-popular notion of colonising Mars was a red herring to the desperate socio-environmental issues Earth faces; a point May wholeheartedly agreed with. They also said 'pioneers' a lot to describe spacefaring adventurers, which is where I got the name for what Karma and Henry were. To this day, and even more so when the pandemic was making such things impossible, I'm kicking myself that I felt too out-of-place in the astronomy scene to talk to Rees afterwards at the signing of his book 'On the Future: Prospects for Humanity'.

Many of the ideas Rees and May explored on-stage – and in Rees' book – made it into my film: the reason for the Pioneers' mission is to find a new world for humanity amidst environmental cataclysm, but they find upon their return that the planet has healed to a point of relative stability; humanity accepting that they must yield to nature for their survival instead of trying to tame it. Meanwhile, the Coetaneous Trust – the private company that funded the mission – now holds a global monopoly. This fuels Karma's conflict: she has lost everything for a mission that was ultimately pointless and the company responsible is now unspeakably better-off. There's a sense of futile injustice, with Karma fighting tooth and nail to make Coetaneous suffer like she has in the vain hope that somehow this can all be put right. But like Einsteinian physics and nature itself, she has no hope of controlling or influencing Coetaneous' corporate gravity.

Now all of this sounds very lovely, but how do you begin shooting this? No matter how much I tried to cook it, you just can't do an Einsteinian space epic in Essex. While developing it, I made a lot of concessions because the ambition just wouldn't be possible otherwise. It would mostly be a two-hander between Karma and Henry, using whatever locations we could find and making the fact that they're ordinary to us – but not to the characters, whose 'present' was an environmental dystopia – seem almost fantastical in an 'appreciate what you have' kind of deal.

In truth, I was bricking it. I was so madly in love with this idea and all the concepts orbiting around it that I didn't want to abandon it because whatever else I could come up with just wouldn't light my passions in the same way, but I also didn't want to do something that wouldn't even come close to what it should be. Plus, no matter how much I tried to take ownership of these concepts and not rely on the song, I felt a massive responsibility to live up to ''39'. No matter how many of these toys I was making myself, it was still Brian May's toy-box and I'd feel a great deal of shame if I turned in something so mediocre because of compromise and a troubled production.

These worries became much more difficult to grapple with when the coronavirus sprung forth in March 2020. Shooting a film may just be a bit too much of an ask during a deadly pandemic… So what could I do? I didn't want it to be a purely theoretical thing where I talked about what I would've done if the pandemic didn't happen, as was being offered at the time – I wanted to actually make a film. This film. I suppose I wanted it all, and I wanted it now.

The all-dominating Zoom format of people talking in their homes to a webcam was never considered.

It would've been very easy to make, yes, but it would've defanged it. Making a film about the future without actually showing what has changed is like building a guitar and forgetting the strings: good on you for gutting out your fireplace, but you kinda missed the whole point of making it. Plus, and this is most important... Everyone else was doing Zoom films, and innovation is always forged in the name of petty contrarianism.

My producer Bee Czapár was ultimately the one who cracked how we would go about making the film. After I said that we could at least make the story as an audio drama, she brought up the idea that we use stock footage as a visual element. While the classes taught by my dissertation supervisor Daniel O'Brien on the different ways Soviet filmmakers like Sergei Eisenstein and Dziga Vertov used film montage to create meaning gave us a good theoretical grounding on how this could work, I also had a back-of-the-head flashback to the video made for ''39' by Simon Lupton and Rhys Thomas. While splicing together footage of the band from Earl's Court 1977 and 2005's 'Return of the Champions' to create a lovely, appropriate feeling of time dilation, Lupton and Thomas also use NASA archive footage of rockets slipping the surly bonds of Earth and astronauts sailing the milky seas: recontextualising this footage to represent the 'volunteers' in ''39's narrative. I thought before the pandemic that, if I really wanted to show a bit of the space journey in passing, I could raid NASA's archive and use similar footage.

I fell in love with the idea of the whole film being a montage like that: the visuals only making sense because of what the audio is doing. Much later, when I sent a rough cut to some people to critique, an American friend said that it was like 'a music video for a radio play,' which I think is the perfect description and a nice hat-tip to its roots. The gist of how the film works is that the narrative – dialogue, sound effects and such – is told completely in audio, while stock footage is used to illustrate what's happening and how the characters are feeling at any moment. For example, the scene where Karma walks into a café to meet up with Henry and their mutual acquaintance Maisie Yaffe would use footage of a café to ground the scene, but then we play a bit with visuals. As Karma acts very prickly to Maisie, footage of a cactus is used when she's being particularly harsh, while Maisie, as a very vibrant person, is shown to be a sunflower. There are a lot more in-depth examples, but I don't want to run the risk of just rewriting my whole dissertation here and this is a good flavour of how it works.

These kinds of dynamics really allowed the film to not be constrained by the pandemic because it shifted the goalposts of what it could be as we really get to dig beneath the surface of these characters and how they see the world they've ended up in. When we shifted to this style, Dan encouraged me to write the script without any of the concessions I had been making so it would be possible to shoot this in live-action, and the result was so liberating. Even though I reasoned that the space journey was the least important part of this story of surviving past a traumatic event, I felt now I would be able to explore it a little bit; to get stolen glances at who these characters were before Special Relativity derailed their lives. It made the impact of who they are now so much greater, and it would have only been possible in this new format. It feels weird and a little dirty to say that COVID-19 made this film better, but it really did. It took it beyond the restraints of a student film and made it into something I'm genuinely proud of.

In the end, because of the pandemic consuming everyone's lives, I had to take on the mantles of writer, director, editor and primary composer. This is an unspeakably bad, borderline apocalyptic idea as you're spread so thin, basically making the whole film yourself, you have to jettison every other aspect of your life to make it on time. I had to manually download over 600 different pieces of stock footage that worked on several metaphorical levels for each bit of dialogue and then stitching/blending them together in a way that flows well. I was mentally exhausted within a few days from doing all of this on my own. I was burnt-out from being burnt-out, and moments like the one I wrote at the start of this essay were filled with never-ending dread... Until I saw, at the end of every sequence, how well it all came together. That kept me going in place of silly things like sleep, friends and food.

My mantra for this film, especially under this new format, was something May said in 2014: "If a thing is worth doing, it's worth overdoing." The uni would have absolutely excused not handing in an actual film in these circumstances, but I wanted to go the extra lightyear, defy all expectations and hand in something so indescribably-crazy that the markers wouldn't have any idea how to feel about it. That's the dream, isn't it? As lovely as it is to make something that's technically brilliant, making something so bonkers that a viewer doesn't know how to feel about it takes up more space in their head because they're trying to figure out just what they watched. My hope was always that viewers would be caught completely off-guard on the first watch and wouldn't know what to make of it, but would really 'get' what the film is doing and understand how it works on a rewatch. It was hysterical to later learn that a third marker needed to come in because the original two were at war with each other over what they thought of it!

While I approached this to stand on its own and not be seen as 'just a Queen film,' it would've been wrong to not put in a couple of nods to its original source of inspiration. I struggled a bit with this aspect because I've experienced horrible gatekeeping in the past on the basis that anything that can be seen as 'fan-work' is only made to appeal to certain egos when you should be 'doing things for yourself,' so for a time I felt a bit apologetic of where this came from. Those gatekeepers are, of course, wrong: I know the things I make are to express my feelings and ideas in the joyous forges of creation and no-one should be made to feel that just because their work is inspired by something means that they are mindless, derivative and only interested in riding coattails.

Nonetheless, I think it's good to keep a healthy balance when it comes to references, because you don't want to deny where something came from, but you also don't want to overshadow the direction you want to take it for the sake of following someone else's vision. For example, 'Karma' was the film's working title and fit many of the themes, but I eventually felt confident enough in what it adds to its inspiration's story without being 'just' a retelling that I arrived at 'The Land That Our Grandchildren Knew'. It's one of my favourite lines from ''39': at once nostalgic but perversely 'wrong'; echoing a longing for home and the impossibility of reaching it, so it fit everything I was exploring in this new story to a tee. I also originally mentioned in dialogue that the Pioneers left Earth 'in the year of '39,' but that felt a bit too heavy-handed so I made it more vague.

Sometimes things just bleed into the writing that you don't really think about until you read it back. The scene at the beginning where Karma is talking about the Pioneers' mission during a news panel and loses her temper with a bigoted pundit took a lot from May's intense debate with Jim Barrington over foxhunting on the 9 July 2015 edition of 'Newsnight'. The frustration at the idea that a 'common sense' fact should be debated to excuse cruelty being perpetuated is the common thread between the two, with Karma shouting out 'you're just a prick, y'know that?", a more PG version of May's frustrated obscenity at the end of his 'Newsnight' debate.

The name of the star system that the Pioneers reach – the Zodiacal Ouroboros – was a nod to the subject of May's PhD, but there's a slightly more deeper meaning at play there: the zodiac signs are used in the Lunar Calendar, and 'ouroboros' represents a cyclical eternity. As such, the name conjures the image of stars and planets forever being reborn; worlds of endless prosperity that humanity could never completely destroy.

But perhaps the most fun – and unplanned! – Queen connection was in casting. Amidst an already-sensational cast of up-and-coming actors – in the lead roles, Kirsty MacMachan brilliantly played the ugly intricacies of Karma's grief, while Henry Burt showcased a powerful sense of wounded obligation plastered with optimism in his character namesake – I was very fortunate to work with Doug Bogie for a cameo role. As many should know, Doug played bass for Queen in 1971, just before they found John Deacon and set off on their global reign. As well as being a brilliant musician and producer, he's also a devastatingly-good voice actor. When I found myself in the situation where I didn't have a voice for Barnaby Morgan Jones – the elderly partner of Karma's daughter, who doesn't believe that she's really her mother – I asked Doug if he would do it. Doug has a nice grit in his voice – very reminiscent of John Hurt or David Warner, who I saw Barnaby as being like – and when he agreed I actually wrote more lines for him because I wanted to showcase more of his acting range. The scene was already very important as it showed how Karma and Henry were moving in different directions in their lives, but his performance really made it sing. Jeez, what an actor.

If I wrote down all my thoughts about this film, it would quite possibly take up this whole book. It was one of the most joyous, intense and fulfilling creative experiences I've ever had, and it felt like the culmination of everything I had discovered, learned and loved over the last decade of my life. Instead, I want to end things off with a little excerpt from the script. This is a monologue from Karma contemplating the cruelty of memory in the situation she cannot escape from. It contains the only 'in-film' reference to the song as it felt light enough to not steal the scene, while also helping build the sense of emotional abandonment Karma feels. Kirsty did such a beautiful job when we quickly recorded this during our lunch break that we all went a bit quiet afterwards. She got it without me having to offer any direction, and it's one of my favourite moments from the film. Hope y'all like it too:

"You know what you've lived through and what's in your imagination, right? They're two different roads. But when you're walking the line between awake and asleep, they start spiralling into each other. For a moment, you believe in your heart that you danced on the moon, or found someone who really saw you for the first time in your life, or – that your wife and daughter are in the next room. That these things were always true... Then poof. The roads untangle and it doesn't matter whether you wake up or sleep, because the joy of fully believing in that new world is gone, like letters written in the sand. That moment is barely a second, but when you're there, it's a beautiful lifetime... And I want to go back."

Those Were The Days Of My Life

Carl Potter

The year was 1974. I was a 13 year old back in the days when you had a bath twice a week and washed your hair in the kitchen sink.

It was a Sunday evening and my mother had the stereo radiogram on, listening to Tom Browne and the top 40 charts. This was a weekly ritual which really was my first introduction to "up-to-date music", instead of having to endure the likes of Elvis Presley on a 78rpm disc, as thick as a roof slate, and as brittle, on the record player. Showing my age now...? Yes, I'm afraid so. I am a fifty seven year old happily married man with three grown up kids and four grandkids.

This particular Sunday, my dad was washing my hair over the kitchen sink, something that I used to hate as he poured the water over my head with a plastic cup, most of it going up my nose as my head was bent over the edge of the sink. I could just hear the radio in the background between me coughing and spluttering as I gasped for breath, thinking any minute now I was going to drown.

Gunpowder, gelatine, dynamite with a laser beam… "What's this, Mam?" I shouted from the kitchen. "It's some group called Queen," she replied, followed by "It's a load of rubbish, it's that heavy metal stuff with twangy guitars and synthesisers."

Well, not to my waterlogged ears it wasn't. This was the best thing I had heard since listening to this "up-to-date music" and my very first introduction to what was going to be something that would still be with me 44 years on.

I was hooked on those lyrics and that "twangy guitar" sound and started listening to the radio in order to hear it again. My parents had little money then and my pocket money wouldn't stretch to buying the record. The more I heard the song, which of course is 'Killer Queen', (and may I add, **NO SYNTHESISERS** were used on the recording, and neither would be for a number of years to come) the more I wanted to know about Queen.

Before the days of internet and computers, it was difficult to find out much about the band. What did they look like, how old were they, how many were in the band, were they all blokes or was there a female with a falsetto voice as the lead vocalist? My questions were answered when they appeared on 'Top Of The Pops' as a last minute stand-in for David Bowie.

Wow, these are different, what a great sound, what a brilliant guitarist, what an amazing voice this male singer had, the fancy clothes, the hair and how it all blended together with the harmonies, this was brilliant. Needless to say my Mam didn't agree, saying, "This isn't music, it's just a blooming noise, look at the state of them."

So I had to make do with catching 'Killer Queen' on the radio, the odd clip on TV, the odd piece in the paper in order to learn more about this band.

It wasn't until early November the following year, when, out of nowhere, the epic single, complete with beelzebubs, galileos, thunderbolts, lightning and most certainly "twangy and very heavy" guitars, burst on to the airwaves, much to my delight. I can remember thinking to myself, "This is Queen, it's them, this is that band again." I was so excited and, like every other listener, confused, amazed, enthralled and bemused by the lyrics, the sound, the voice, the opera, the length of the song... I just couldn't get enough of it, neither could the great British public as 'Bo Rhap' stormed to number 1 and stayed there for what seemed like an eternity. Fortunately, I had some spare pocket money and remember cycling into York city centre, to Woolworths to buy the single.

That was it. The stereo radiogram never had it so good as at every opportunity I played it over and over again. Before I went to school, in my dinner break, after school, after tea, my mother still objecting profusely.

I couldn't wait for 'Top Of The Pops' and when the video was unveiled, as the number one smash ended the programme, I was left astonished and smiling with glee. As the weeks went by even my mam was starting to warm to them (but she would never freely admit to it).

On Christmas Eve the same year my mam and dad went to the Working Men's Club, as was the in thing back in the day, to start their Christmas celebrations, leaving me at home to look after my younger brother and sister. I rifled through the TV Times Christmas edition, the only time of year it was ever bought, to see what was on the box. I could not believe it when I saw advertised on BBC2, 'Queen Live at The Hammersmith Odeon'. I was made up, parents out, Christmas Eve, younger ones in bed waiting for Santa and the TV to myself.

What an evening viewing that was. After only ever hearing two songs by this new, fresh, charismatic flamboyant group, I was treated to what would become some of the biggest rock standards of all time and indeed one of the best concerts. It was one of the best Christmas Eve's I had ever had and to top it all, on Christmas Day morning my parents had bought me a Binatone portable cassette player and the cassette of 'A Night At The Opera' for Christmas.

That was just the start of it. I used to earn my pocket money by cleaning the bedrooms once a week and every weekend I carried out my chores carting the cassette player from one room to the next playing Queen over and over again until I practically wore out the tape. I managed to get a part-time job stacking shelves at a local supermarket and as soon as the money started coming in I was able to save up and start collecting the back catalogue of Queen albums. I signed up for the 'New Musical Express' from my local newsagents and had it delivered on a weekly basis. Although I did find it a heavy read, it did keep me up to date with what was happening in the world of Queen, although if I recall, the NME weren't big Queen fans. I also joined the Official International Queen Fan Club and always waited in anticipation for the quarterly mag and handwritten letter from each member of the band to drop through the letterbox.

I can always remember eagerly awaiting the release of 'A Day At The Races' and recall taking it to school to listen to it in the art class, a fairly relaxed and chilled lesson where you could bring music in to listen to.

It was from then that my devotion to Queen grew and grew to collect anything I could afford and get hold of. I bought my own Hitachi music centre, from the Co-Op department store on hire purchase and had it on my bedroom cabinet, mounting the speakers in the corners of the wall on brackets. Homework became a little more enjoyable and soon as I had done it, I cranked up the volume and just laid on my bed, following the lyrics from the sleeve notes, playing my air guitar and drums and reading every small detail on the album covers. I bought a red embroidered iron on "Queen" patch for the back of my Levi's denim jacket and thought I was the dogs!

As you can imagine, by this time my mother was tearing her hair out with all this "heavy twangy guitar music" rattling my bedroom floorboards, "Turn it down!" being the regular yell from downstairs.

By the time I got married and left home in 1980, my collection included every album from Queen up to 'Flash Gordon', including 'Live Killers', which blew me away. I was desperate to see this band live and the long wait was over in 1982, when, after the release of 'Hot Space', at Elland Road in Leeds, I was treated to my first live performance of Freddie and the boys, supported by Teardrop Explodes, Heart and Joan Jett and the Blackhearts. The excitement at seeing them live was something I had never experienced before and I was not disappointed. I didn't have one of the best seats in the house but it didn't spoil the experience for me. A long and lasting memory, still with me today.

The concert coincided with a visit to York by the Pope and maybe, unbeknown to the remaining members of the band, hundreds of Queen fans were left stranded on Leeds railway station, as the trains back to York had been cancelled for security reasons. It was a very uncomfortable night trying to get my head down on a rolled up denim jacket, complete with embroidered Queen patch, and a carrier bag with programme and tour T-shirt in it.

Having flown the roost, it was now my younger brother's turn to take over from where I had left off. Having had his ears perfectly honed into the unique sound of Queen, by repetitive renditions of every album he heard from my bedroom, he also became an avid fan. I recorded all the albums I had onto blank cassettes for him, (sorry Queen, it was illegal, I know!) much to the delight (?) of my mother who thought she had heard the end of it. In fact what she did was write a letter to the Queen Fan Club telling the story of my obsession with the band, leaving home, thinking that she could be left in peace, only for my kid brother to do exactly the same. Jacky at the fan club was so amused and touched by the letter our mam had written in, that she arranged for two personally autographed, with our names on them, photographs of Freddie to be posted out. You can imagine the surprise and delight that this brought to my brother and I as she proudly gave them to us at a family gathering of some description. To this day we both have those signed photos, although my original has faded due to sunlight and many, many years of a prime spot on the front room wall in every house I have lived in since. My father-in-law is a keen photographer and has recently managed to replicate the photo, enhancing the colours and adding some text, so my name and Freddie's signature is still there to see, and I still have the original upstairs.

Every Queen album, video, DVD, book, magazine, boxset, and as much memorabilia that I could afford, and that my wife would allow me to buy, has been collected over the years. A ticket to the Works Tour at Wembley arena in 1984, the Magic Tour at Wembley stadium in '86 (second night) the Freddie tribute concert in '92 after the untimely passing of the greatest man. Annual trips to Garden Lodge on 24 November – always wet, windy and freezing – and visits to the "Old Bakehouse" HQ of the original fan club. A surprise trip to Montreux for my fortieth birthday. A personally designed full back piece tattoo of the band and the crest, which won best in show at a tattoo convention in Blackpool. Brian May concerts, Roger Taylor concerts, tribute band concerts, 'We Will Rock You' in London, Queen & Paul Rogers, QUEX and 2 Q&AL concerts. One in Sheffield 2017 and most recently in Barcelona, my adoration for their music, live performance and total respect for Brian and Roger I still share to this day.

Unfortunately, our good old mam passed away last year after a long illness which eventually led to dementia depriving her the chance to see two of her four great-grandkids. The youngest, one year old this December, named after the great pretender himself, Freddie.

I had always wanted a 'man cave' or bar-type construction in my garden, something which I had been mulling over for a while. I was given "permission" by my good lady wife in the form of a gift on Christmas Day 2014. It was a certificate scroll that she had typed up, accompanied with a hammer-cum-icepick. That was all I needed and in the spring of 2015, I started to demolish the old garden shed in order to make way for my bespoke building.

Having just about cleared the area and having seen a wooden sports bar on the internet, my project came to a sudden halt. On a bright sunny evening in June, I was knocked off my push bike by a car that headed straight towards me on my side of the road. I was on my way home from work and suffered serious head and facial injuries, three fractured ribs, two broken vertebrae and cuts and bruises all over. Luckily I am still here to tell the tale, making a full recovery, but delaying my project for nearly a year.

Autumn 2015 we got the landscapers in to re-plan the garden paths and build the decked area that was to form the base for my bar. 2016 came and as soon as the weather brightened up I ordered the sports bar and my project began. October saw its official naming ceremony and installation of a last orders bell, and the bar was established in 2016, although a very long way off completion. Covered in tarpaulin I managed to work through the winter, dark nights and inclement weather making my vision gradually turn to reality. In May 2017, I invited friends and family round for an "official" opening and unveiling of my DIY handiwork.

I had draped decorating sheets around the front and side. I had purchased a smoke machine and had flashing lights, music and all the glitz of an opening to a Queen gig. The widescreen TV was paused at the opening of the Magic gig at Wembley Stadium, the twin towers and 'One Vision' ready to play through the surround sound as my masterpiece was unveiled by my son and son-in-law. As Freddie launched onto the stage, I launched out of my bar, complete in Freddie outfit and strutted my stuff around the back garden much to the amusement of my audience and neighbours. A fantastic afternoon was had by all, the bar had been christened and 'Kurgan's Korner' was declared officially and finally open.

Thanks to my lovely wife, my family, my late mam, Tom Browne and the inspiration of the greatest rock band that will ever walk the planet, my dream had become a reality. I had excelled even my own expectations, building more of a themed pub than just a wooden bar.

As I write this now, the project is still work in progress, my wife and I moving pictures, making adjustments, adding things to the collection of Queen, holiday and family trinkets. Will it ever be finished? I don't know, but we have had some great times in it since its construction.

I am just short of a 'mini-May' guitar to take pride of place inside it and have been throwing out subtle hints to the family as my birthday and Christmas approach. Perhaps when, or if, I get one, Brian and Roger may pay me a visit when they find themselves in this neck of the woods? A cup of Yorkshire Tea for Brian and a nice cold Bierre Moretti for Roger will be waiting. In return for a couple of autographs, of course, my darlings!

By no means do I profess to be the biggest Queen fan in the world. There are some out there who have travelled the earth, bought everything possible and gone to extremes in order to follow our idols and I take my hat off to you all. I am simply an ageing, grey-haired, bespectacled old rocker wanting to share 44 years of my life and experiences as a modest, but dedicated Queen fan.

"It's been no bed of roses, no pleasure cruise, but I thank you all."

Queen - A Covers Band

Richard Hearn

Long before their album of 1986, the front covers of Queen albums evoked a kind of magic (pun intended). A band whose music twisted through genres and re-inventions had covers which reflected this variety. Many of these covers have become iconic; some have even performed The Miracle (okay, just assume all puns are intended) of making a patchy album seem – at least on the surface – cohesive.

For those of you who believe that you should never judge a book – or album – by its cover, feel free to skip / lift and replace the needle (delete as applicable).

Maybe I'm more superficial, easily led, but let me take you through the covers of the fifteen studio albums. Not in chronological order – what's good enough for the film 'Bohemian Rhapsody' is good enough for me – instead, I'm going to take you on my own personal journey, through the Queen albums in the order I bought them.

Let's start, as all love stories should start, with a Venn diagram. The first circle's got the single 'Save Me' in it, bought at the age of 9, my version a strangely warped 7" which exaggerated the see-sawing melody. The second overlapping circle is the opening synthesisers of 'Play the Game', repeatedly played on the radio during a never-ending caravan journey in 1980. When I realised it was the same band, and then saw the third circle

– 'The Game' in cassette form like a silver cigarette box (an aspirational image for a child that's dated badly) – I was hooked.

Their leather jackets and serious expressions made it look like their heaviest, rockiest album of all. In fact, the Queen doth protest too much, and it was the perfect fusion of Queen's '70s harmonies with a new funk influence. Not that I thought this aged nine; I just liked the tunes.

So I decided to spend all my pocket money slowly accumulating what older albums I could get my hands on. Next up was 'A Day At The Races'. Despite the album title, it has a dark – yes, alright, black – background, with mysterious beasts. The cover, and the warm, shadow-filled, ethereal nature of songs such as 'You Take My Breath Away' and 'The Millionaire Waltz' evoke the atmosphere of 'A Midsummer Night's Dream'.

Likewise, it's the white background, rather than the title of 'A Night At The Opera' that pinpoints its mood. We're at the circus, I'd say, rather than the opera, a matinee, with an extraordinary set of excellent acts, book-ended and interval'd appropriately. The crest – and Queen's name – reflects their high aspirations, essentially saying we've been here a while, and we're here to say.

A side-memory: The cassette version I had of 'Opera' didn't come with lyrics. So, if you were obsessed as me, you had to press pause every three seconds to transcribe the lyrics into a small exercise book bought especially for the purpose. This was my misspent youth; my Mum calling me down for my jam roly-poly while I'm scribbling 'A sewer rat decaying in a... IN A MINUTE, MUM!... Cesspool of Pride... Coming!"

Next up in my time-hopping journey was Queen's debut album. Is this the outlier in all their covers, with Freddie the only band member featuring? It's a tribute to their democracy that from then on, they're either not on the cover, or all given equal prominence. Still, it's a great image, with Freddie's stage persona quite literally to the forefront, recognised from Day One as a key USP.

Next up, 'Queen II', a cover that exudes confidence and sets the tone perfectly. (You'd get them on the Trade Descriptions Act if they'd still been called Smile). Symmetry, shadows, they're literally looking down their nose at us. And by the end of the album, you know they're right to. They are better than us, they're gods, deserving of all the adulation. Any album that has the line 'blue-powder monkeys playing in the dead of night' and still feel like it's speaking direct to me, just me, is surely The Best.

The 'Sheer Heart Attack' cover is a more earthy vibe. A reaction perhaps. We were dispassionately cool on the previous album, think Queen, let's go for 'hot' on this one, lads. Not as in sexy, necessarily, more like... could someone open a window? Maybe they're just showing solidarity with Brian, as he's feverish from the hepatitis he contracted at this time. They've all generously gone for the same look, like when you paint the whole living room to match the damp patch.

Fast forward past 'Races' and 'Opera' and we're well into the future, or at least the past's (50s) vision of the future (not sure exact decade) and re-hashed in the '70s. Still with me? Often voted a fan's favourite cover – and apparently Roger's – it's perhaps a reaction to the self-consciously regal crest of 'Races' and 'Opera'. Perhaps bridling at their establishment reputation, it reverses the power balance to depict them not just as the underdog, but at the mercy of an oversized robot. Just like 'News of the World's two anthemic openers, its pulp sci-fi feel has the finger on the popular pulse; I'd use the phrase 'crowd pleaser' except the crowd in the gatefold inner looks to be running for their lives.

'Jazz' follows what I call The Rule of the England Manager. Always ricochet to the opposite option, so the retro-illustration of 'News Of The World' morphs into the overtly graphic design of 'Jazz' (apparently inspired by an image on the Berlin Wall). Does it suit the album? Not at all. Does it matter? Not at all. "It's stark, it's simple, it intrigues, it's understated," Roger probably said. "Love it," says Brian. "Now if we just put a row of naked women on bicycles along the edges, we've got our final design".

'Flash Gordon' simply, er... flashes... the name like lightening across the cover. It's bold, it's dramatic. But nighttime – where lightning normally resides – would be too... dark. Let's have a daytime yellow, but not a real yellow, because it's not a realistic film, instead a basic spectrum yellow straight out of the tin, as artificial as cheap custard, and just as pleasing. The cover of Gordon's very much alive.

Leapfrog the already-covered 'The Game' (remember, that was my origin story) into 'Hot Space'. I recall seeing it, just released, in a record shop in Croydon. It was a complete surprise, the sort of surprise no fan has had since the age of the internet. If I ever have a dream where something unexpectedly great is stumbled upon, then this, yes this, is what it reminds me of. Personally, it's my favourite album cover. (Stop throwing things, and let me explain). It's striking, but also perfectly representative of where they were at the time. Each in their own geometrical box, echoing their alleged separateness during this period. Their heads are reduced to distinctive features. Freddie's moustache. Brian's big hair. Roger's rock star good looks. John's also there. I jest, of course. John's influence is all over this album. It's a great cover to an underrated album. I admire their attempt at reinvention. It didn't always work, but that doesn't make me admire it less.

'The Works' cover is again a deliberate reaction, this time to the critical response of 'Hot Space'. It's a cover that screams we're a safe pair of hands, we're not going to frighten the horses. Look, we're even sitting down. There's a sepia tinge too, as if they're saying 'we get it, let's go back to the past'. Even if, with tracks like 'Radio Ga Ga' and 'I Want To Break Free', some of the 'Hot Space' DNA has been retained.

Between 'The Works' and 'A Kind of Magic', Live Aid happened. Their wider popularity (demonstrated by their accompanying stadium-filling Magic Tour) led to a distinctly family-friendly, mainstream aesthetic. They're a dancing, cartoon version of themselves, like something off a cereal packet, and certainly the cheeriest anyone's ever looked publicising music from a film about beheadings. Inflatables of their cover personas floated off above Wembley. Thank God, purely for this reason, they never did tour 'The Miracle'. A giant version of that landing in your back garden would have given you PTSD for years.

Yes, 'The Miracle' cover. It's a freakshow which you can't take your eyes off (and the back cover can't take its eyes off you). I was always told it was rude to stare. Meant, I think, to represent their supposed songwriting unity, though, in retrospect it feels like a 'unity' thrashed out by Intellectual Property lawyers. It looks like something genetically-modified left on a hob, and you can't quite work out where the joins are. Brightly-lit and slightly unpleasant. Yes, it does fit well with the music.

'Innuendo' therefore comes as a relief. Born of necessity perhaps, as photos of the band might ask too many questions about Freddie's health, we go from too much face on 'The Miracle' to no faces at all on 'Innuendo'. It's a great looking album, with atmosphere and attention to detail and – certainly after the last two covers – a certain enigmatic quality. Again, it matches the music, a return to form.

Finally, 'Made in Heaven'. If you like this cover, you're probably going to like the album. In a recent 'Record Collector' magazine, where fans submitted questions, I asked what their favourite covers were. Roger went for 'News of the World' as previously mentioned. Brian went for 'Made in Heaven', calling it 'abstract'. Who am I to argue with the great man, especially on a project which must have been soaked in emotion. However, is it in fact too literal? Straining hard for symbolism and, excusably in the circurmstances, too sentimental? Freddie's statue on one side, and the remaining three on the other, reminds me of that optical illusion with a bird and a cage on opposite sides of a card. Spin it quick enough and they appear together, just like the music attempts the same trick, with guitar solos and added harmonies pretending everyone's in the same room. Sometimes less is more.

To the last, though, the covers are a fantastic reflection of their musical evolution. They tell their own visual story to complement the audio; changing styles, the serious next to the playful, frequently iconic, instantly recognisable, always striking, and utterly Queen.

Just like their music!

Hope And Glory: My Life Through Queen

Fiona Nicholas

I met Freddie Mercury about 1973 at the tender age of 13. It was at the railway station in Portsmouth. I plonked myself next to him not realising who it was. He said hello and started talking to me. I was terrified, as an awkward teenager I grunted some sort of answer back. Oh, how I regret not being more responsive!

I then went on to see Queen at Southampton, with my older brother, he had taken me to many gigs. I was absolutely blown away, never had I experienced anything so exciting ever, the sound, enthusiasm, such exceptional talent, and of course the wonderful charismatic Freddie. From that day I was hooked and never looked back.

Then some years later went to see them in Brighton. I was surprised at Freddie's new look, not sure if I liked it at first; love it in the end. But another awesome show, you never get disappointed by Queen. The lights, the anticipation, only to be in more awe again.

Then the final show at Knebworth, the huge crowd, the electric atmosphere, them flying over in the helicopter. The sheer (almost unbearable) excitement of the build up then they were on WOW! I feel so lucky to have been there.

I was at the Goodwood Festival of Speed, staring inside the window of a Jenson Interceptor. Opposite me through the other front window a head and voice popped up saying what a wonderful car it was. It was Roger Taylor thankfully I had much more to say that time around!

I have been very fortunate enough to visit Zanzibar twice, visiting the birth place of Freddie Mercury, his school and the house he was born and lived in Stone Town. I've also stayed at Tembo House Hotel, where he used to go swimming with his family. It seems strange when you are there, that a young man from such an exotic faraway country fitted in so well with London life. They have a bar/restaurant called Mercury's there with some fantastic photos of Queen, with Queen blaring out of the speakers, overlooking the sea on this exotic paradise island.

The funniest thing was when I arrived in Zanzibar the hotel manager showed me a picture of Freddie, then explained he was the lead singer of a band called Queen, to which he asked if I had heard of them – so I politely asked him if they had any success. Couldn't help myself.

Four years ago, I decided to travel to Montreux, to see the iconic statue overlooking Lake Geneva and the Queen studio experience. It was fabulous.

I feel Queen have been with me through my life with their fantastic diverse music. But this next story really gets, the power and influence their music has touched so many people not only on the fantastic fans but *EVERYONE*.

Through the 2020 pandemic from March to July, at work we were allowed to play music to cheer us and the customers up, in the small shop I work in.

So Queen was the choice of all the staff, with ages ranging from seventeen to sixty. We had 'Bohemian Rhapsody' blaring out. My work friends and I all trying to do the harmonies shop (badly, I expect), from different corners of the shop.

The customers are all joining in singing loudly, from the socially distanced queues inside and outside the shop, from nine-year-olds to eighty-plus. It seemed the song was giving us all hope and joy for the future. It was very emotional.

I suppose it was the equivalent of the Italians doing opera from their balconies.

Thank you, Queen, for the past, present and future.

Aura(l) Pleasures – Queen's 'Flash Gordon' Soundtrack

Don Klees

All that's missing is the images – until you realise the music has already sketched them for you. Very few movie scores evoke the film they accompany more intimately than Queen's soundtrack for 'Flash Gordon'. Likewise, there are very few artists whose musical personality fits a movie better than Queen's did with this one. The match is all the more striking considering that the band was neither impresario Dino De Laurentis nor director Mike Hodges' first choice to provide the soundtrack.

Behind-the-scenes intrigue aside, choosing Queen – then nearing the peak of their pre-Live Aid popularity – to score the movie spoke to its commercial ambitions in no uncertain terms. Coming just a few years after the original 'Star Wars' and the first Christopher Reeve 'Superman' movie, both of which owed some debt to earlier incarnations of its source material, 'Flash Gordon' was clearly envisioned as a potential blockbuster – perhaps the start of a "franchise" in contemporary terms. However, despite a respectable box-office performance, especially in the UK, it ultimately took its place in the realm of cult classics.

In that respect, the movie and its soundtrack are well matched. By soundtrack album standards, it was quite successful, reaching the top 10 in several countries and the top 30 in several more. By Queen standards, though, the record fell short of the more traditional albums that came before and after. The next time the group embraced movie music in earnest, the focus was individual songs rather than a score, making 'Flash Gordon' a cult classic within the band's body of work.

This holds true for both the music and its presentation. Several years ago The Guardian's music critic, Alexis Petridis suggested that, "If [Flash Gordon's] instrumentals weren't covered in dialogue, it's tempting to think they would be afforded the same hipster reverence as Giorgio Moroder and Vangelis." He added that, "Overlooking the opportunity to heavily feature the sound of Brian Blessed shouting his head off wouldn't have been very Queen." While the latter point is accurate, it also underestimates the album's accomplishment.

"We wanted to do something that was a real soundtrack," Queen guitarist Brian May told 'Melody Maker' in 1980. May's comment was intended to contrast the "toned down" efforts of other rock artists to write music for movies with the autonomy Queen had to be themselves, "as long as it complemented the picture." Though the band reputedly only watched a rough 20-minute segment of the movie before starting work on the soundtrack, they clearly saw their own pop-art inclinations reflected in it.

That affinity isn't surprising since the movie's script was written by Lorenzo Semple Jr., one of the architects of the pop-art influenced 'Batman' TV series from the 1960s. As in 'Batman', the leads in 'Flash Gordon' mainly serve as earnest embodiments of virtue allowing the renowned actors around them to shine as the larger-than-life supporting characters. Brian Blessed is the most iconic example, but Timothy Dalton, Max Von Sydow and Peter Wyngarde all get a share of the spotlight. The soundtrack's particular triumph is weaving those performances into the music in such a way that it recaptures the experience of the movie for listeners.

From the vantage point of an overloaded, on-demand, viewing environment, it's easy to forget just how few avenues existed to revisit a favourite movie or TV series in the years before VCRs became commonplace. Novelisations, comics and View-Master all offered individual engagement, but none of these mediums were especially immersive. Even with large sections of dialogue from the movie and excerpts from John Williams' score, the narrated record 'The Story Of Star Wars' simply recounted the movie's events rather than allowing them to envelop listeners.

In contrast, the opening scene with Ming the Merciless and Klytus brings listeners into the 'Flash Gordon' world within moments of putting the needle down on the record (or the digital equivalent). From there the album uses dialogue sparingly to convey mood and feeling more so than plot. This means some favourite lines are absent – namely Prince Barin's epic exclamation, "Freeze, you bloody bastards!" – but the overall effect is worth it. The takeaway from any beloved movie tends to be emotional rather than intellectual, a function of texture as much as text.

Queen's music is a fundamental part of the texture of 'Flash Gordon'. From propulsive pieces like 'Battle Theme', which accompanies the Hawkmen attack, to more delicate interludes such as 'Execution of Flash', it's virtually impossible to imagine the onscreen scenes could exist without the band's contributions. In the former, the incorporation of some well-chosen dialogue ensures that Brian Blessed as Prince Vultan both steals and embodies the show. With his mix of being serious about what he does but not necessarily how he does it. Vultan can be seen as Queen's onscreen avatar. Whatever the band's intentions in that area, his presence certainly makes the soundtrack more compelling.

The same applies to the single version of 'Flash's Theme'. As expertly crafted as any of Queen's other hits, 'Flash' distills the album's approach into an exquisite two minutes and forty-eight seconds of pop-music pleasure. Like the album, it didn't reach the same heights as many other Queen releases, but the inclusion of Vultan saying "Gordon's alive" turned that line into a catchphrase that Brian Blessed still obligingly performs for fans.

Had 'Flash Gordon' been a huge hit, with the soundtrack becoming one of the best-selling albums of Queen's career, it's tempting to wonder if the band would have revisited that world for the inevitable sequels. Could they have found fresh inspiration or would the law of diminishing returns – exemplified by the Bee Gees' soundtrack for 'Staying Alive' – have taken hold? That thought aside, the actual circumstances are perfect in their own way. In a franchise-driven world, the movie and album are twin testaments to the value of one-offs, an artful fusion of sound and vision that continues to thrill.

*Originally published in **We Are Cult**, 24 August 2018.*

Peter Freestone Interview

Peter "Phoebe" Freestone was Freddie Mercury's faithful personal assistant, living and travelling alongside him for many years.

Peter, you were working for the Royal Ballet when you first met Freddie, were you aware of Queen at that time?

Yes, because this was 1979 and I knew 'Seven Seas of Rhye', 'Killer Queen' and 'Bohemian Rhapsody'. That was my total knowledge of Queen. Although, I think it would have been 1973, I did actually see Freddie Mercury in the flesh when I was having tea in Biba and he walked in with Mary [Austin]. So, yes, I knew that Queen existed.

Were you into that kind of music?

Queen wasn't really my kind of music; it wasn't the music I listened to.

What kind of music were you into at that time?

Classical! That's why working at the Opera House was perfect. I got paid to listen to music, the best performers in the world!

What was it like going from the Royal Ballet and into the world of Queen and rock music, did that take some adjusting to?

Yes and no. The thing is, the job itself was actually fairly similar, except in the Royal Ballet it was five of us looking after fifty people. With Queen there was one of me looking after four. Basically, though, the job was the same. You had to have the costumes ready to put them on, take them off, get them clean and get them ready for the next show. With Queen it was a little bit different because you didn't know from one night to the next exactly what they would want to be wearing, so you had to have everything ready for them. At the Royal Ballet, you knew what show was going on, you knew what costumes had to be ready and who was in, because you saw the cast list in the morning for the evening. So, you got those costumes ready. The job itself was fairly similar, except of course it was a different venue each night with Queen. After the first tour, things changed a little bit because I got to know Freddie in those six weeks. Then he invited me out for dinner and we met up in between that tour and the next tour and the relationship had changed.

What were your first impressions of the band members?

Well, the first thing I ever thought when I saw Freddie, when I was first introduced to him was, "Hmm… He's not very tall, is he?" Because he was 5ft 9 and I was 6ft 2.

I first saw the whole band together at the first rehearsal I went to. This was for The Crazy Tour. It was at Borehamwood or Pinewood, I can't remember which, but it was one of those film studios in West London. I was shown the costume trunks and Paul Prenter said "Once the band have arrived, I'll introduce you and you can talk, see what they want", that sort of stuff. So, I was with the costume trunks and I kept looking and I saw all these people arriving. I didn't see anybody who looked like a famous rock star! The only person that looked anything like your image of a rock star was this person who just strutted in, wearing a shoulder to floor length wolfskin coat. I thought "Well has to be one of them" but, no, that was [Queen's manager] Jim Beach. The rest of the band were just... ordinary mortals! [laughs] That was the thing that struck me, not one of them had any of the airs and graces or the "Don't you know who I am?" attitude. This is the thing I have learned over years with Freddie, real stars can be the nicest people on Earth. It's the wannabes, the ones who never quite made it, who need to be "I'm a star! You must treat me properly!". The people who really worked hard, they can often be the humblest and most generous people you could ever meet.

You spent a lot of time with Queen at the recording studios, what was that like?

I was with them more in the beginning than in the end. The last couple of albums were recorded in London, Townhouse or Metropolis studios and Freddie would go with Terry [Giddings, Freddie's driver] and someone else might go. In the beginning I was there for quite a lot of the stuff. It could be incredibly boring. The crew had a job to do, they had to make sure all the instruments were there and everything was working properly. I would just be hanging around making drinks, getting food sorted out, that sort of thing. I remember in Musicland Studios; I would be in the kitchen; I would get the food ready.

When you think, I was actually in the room when some of the most amazing things were created, 'Under Pressure', for example. In Los Angeles, Rod Stewart was singing on a couple of tracks, you know, just messing around. I was there when Freddie was working with Michael Jackson. I was present for most of 'Barcelona'. I was there for some of the most incredible creations but when it's happening, it doesn't feel like that. You hear little bits of this, little bits of that and you think "That sounds like there could be something there" but it doesn't turn out like anything you imagined it to be but it turns out incredibly well.

Can I ask you about the 'Under Pressure' sessions with David Bowie, what was that like?

It was accidental, really. The band were in the studio and [producer] David Richards called David Bowie and said, "Come down, you're in town, why not?". Of course, David Bowie knew them anyway and then they started messing around. John had come up with this riff, the bassline and they went from there. They worked solidly for hours and hours, then went out for something to eat and they couldn't remember what they'd done when they came back! [laughs] Then of course they started playing with the tapes and it came back.

There's the famous story of how the vocal tracks were done. David came up with the idea that Freddie should go into the studio to record what he felt and David wouldn't be around. Then David would go into the studio and record what he felt and see where they could meet in the middle. So basically, Freddie went into the studio and started singing and David Bowie was standing outside listening to what Freddie did. He went in and sort of copied Freddie. So, Freddie thought "Oh wow! We're thinking exactly the same! It's incredible!". And then, of course, he found out. They called each other names, you know, in humour. Then they took the master to New York. David had to go to New York and the track wasn't finished, but they had decided it was worth finishing. Freddie, Mack and I went to New York with the master track and spent twenty-four hours putting the last vocal on.

So, when Freddie had come up with a new track, did you sense the excitement in him?

Yes! The thing is, you have to also remember though, he had already created some amazing tracks. Of course, the one the whole world remembers is 'Bohemian Rhapsody'. But listening to 'Killer Queen' which was in itself was unheard of in those days and the other one that I knew, 'Seven Seas Of Rhye', you look at 'In the Lap Of The Gods (Revisited)' and you look at Freddie's favourite track of everything he ever did, 'Somebody To Love', for him it was much more of a daily occurrence. He really expected himself to be able to write something amazing, something brilliant.

What is your favourite memory of Freddie performing live?

Probably the one that I wasn't there at. For me, the best live show I have ever seen and that was obviously on film, was the Budapest show [1986].

There was just something about that show. I was not, at that point, really a Queen fan. I didn't become a fan until about 1995.

Wow!

Well, the thing is, you couldn't do the work and be a fan.

I get what you mean, because you were just surrounded by it all the time weren't you?

Yes! You just stand there, doing nothing with your mouth open. You could not be a fan and do the job and it wasn't until 1995 that I really sat down and started listening to the music. When I started on the book ['Freddie Mercury' by Peter Freestone, published in 1999 by Omnibus Press] I actually listened to all the music and watched all the videos. Then I actually saw how much more there was to all this music.

I have to say that the Blu-ray release of that concert just looks fantastic.

Yeah! For me, it's held some sort of magic. Maybe because of the venue. Maybe for them, being behind the Iron Curtain, even though it was sort of hanging quite loosely at that point in Hungary, but, you know, doing something that they'd never done before. It brought back some of the feeling of South America, doing that first stadium tour.

You could sense they were excited about it on the little film inserts.

This is it. There was absolutely nothing run of the mill.

What do you recall about the day of Live Aid?

I remember how at ease Freddie was with everyone who was there. Before they had done anything, it was this amazing show and everyone who was going on, they were 'the best so far!' and all of that. For Freddie, it was one of the rare chances he got to spend time with his peers. He did not spend time at rock concerts, he didn't go to gigs, he didn't do that sort of thing. He liked opera, ballet, theatre. So, he got to spend time with people at Live Aid. There's that well known picture of him sitting with Adam Ant and Roger and of course, one with him and Elton. He was actually really quite relaxed because they had rehearsed. They had spent three or four days rehearsing, so he wasn't worried about it. Until he actually got on the stage, he wasn't thinking of the enormity of the show. Of course, in his head, he knew he was playing to the world because of the cameras and everything. Then he got on the stage and the atmosphere in the stadium and seeing the crowd… normally they would only see the first ten rows. So, seeing the whole stadium full, I think that is what charged him. Freddie was one of these artists, he would give to the audience but the more they gave back, the more he would give them. You couldn't have had a better audience than they had at Live Aid.

At the time I was eleven years old watching it on TV, and Queen's performance had more of an effect on me than most of the concerts that I've actually been to. I remember some of the artists before Queen had seemed a bit aloof and had not really interacted with the audience. Freddie came on and it wasn't a case of 'us and them', he took the audience with him all the way.

That was his job. His job, always, and Brian has said this in interviews, Freddie's job was to grab the audience from the second he went on to the stage. He was there to get the attention of every single person in the audience. As I say, they had rehearsed so they didn't have to think about what they were doing. They just went onstage to give a show. I don't know if any other people in America or the UK actually rehearsed for Live Aid. So many people, when they do these charity shows, they think, "Oh well, we're only going to go on and sing a couple of songs. What do we have to rehearse for?" and it shows in their performance. So, when Queen went on, they were at ease on the stage and then could concentrate on giving a show. Also, they didn't have to think about saving energy or anything. They had twenty minutes. So, you could put all of the energy of an hour and a half show into twenty minutes. Then he was going to have a couple of hours rest before he had to go and sing one more song. That also had an effect. They could just throw themselves into it.

How did Freddie go from an event like Live Aid, with that amount of energy and crowd adoration, to just sitting at home or whatever the next day?

This is why he was out all night after a show. There was absolutely no point in going straight to a hotel or straight back home. What would he do if he did that? He'd be just hitting his head on the walls. So that's why he was out all night, just to get rid of the adrenalin.

He did it on tour as well. I cannot remember one night where he didn't. Well, there was one night where he did, but he didn't go back to a hotel, he went to the hospital. After he damaged his knee in Munich and they were on the European Tour, his knee gave way in Hanover. He had to be carried offstage and then he was carried back on, they did four or five more songs at the piano and he was taken straight to the hospital.

When Freddie was at home, did he have a big record collection and was he into having a really decent stereo system?

He had a sort of quality sound system, he had someone put it all together, "He should have this, he should have that, he should have something else" and they came in and installed it. As far as a record collection went, no. Not at all.

That surprises me.

He listened to Prince. Although, he watched Prince rather than listened to him. He would get videos. He would just sit and watch that. You see, in the end, for him music was his work. It was his business side. The work side. Whether it was recording, creating or performing. Home was for relaxing, home was for his private life, his outside of work life. He never, ever had anything like a microphone there. I don't know how he would record nowadays where everyone records at home and then takes it to the studio, mix it and then take it home again, you know? The studio was where he created his music, that was his office.

If Freddie was having a quiet night in at Garden Lodge, what was that like? Did he have favourite TV shows for example?

Well, he would have an afternoon in! [laughs] He would watch 'Countdown'. He LOVED 'Countdown'.

Well, he loved words, didn't he?

Yes, he loved words but he hated the numbers part. He loved the letters part. He didn't watch soaps; he didn't watch those sorts of things really. He would watch comedy shows, 'Alas Smith & Jones' and that sort of stuff.

Let's talk about Monserrat Caballe. It must have been an amazing moment when she came to Garden Lodge?

It was so, so amazing! We were at the recital and then Freddie ran off home to get changed and ready, so I waited with Monserrat at the Opera House and brought her back when she had changed and signed her autographs. We sat, we had something to eat and then from twelve, maybe one o'clock through to six o'clock in the morning, they were just around the piano. They were laughing, singing, performing. Everything and anything. It was just so natural.

Freddie was so worried because Monserrat had to catch a flight at nine o'clock in the morning. She had done a show the night before. He didn't want her tired. She was taking cigarettes out of his packet. He said, "You can't smoke! You can't smoke! Your voice!" He said, "What are you doing?". It was like two old friends having an evening in.

You could tell when they were being interviewed together that the respect was mutual.

Yes! Very, very much so. As far as Freddie was always concerned, she had the best voice in the world. There was nothing that was ever going to take that away and for Monserrat, Freddie was THE greatest performer. He could perform physically and vocally.

Had Freddie lived, I would have loved to have heard Freddie explore the opera stuff some more.

Oh, he would have done! I'm sure Queen would have carried on; the music would keep coming out. I doubt very much whether he would be on stage now. He was always laughing when The Rolling Stones were going out on another tour and The Who were going out on another tour, all these pensioners going out on the road. He would always say, "Why put yourself there for people to laugh at you?".

What did you think of The Freddie Mercury Tribute Concert?

Well, apparently, it was only George Michael who sang in the original key, which says something. Freddie never claimed to have the highest voice in rock. He was always so, so envious of... You remember the rock of the eighties?

Yes!

The American rock... you know, Foreigner, etc., they all had these tenor voices singing their hearts out. He was so jealous of them because he didn't have that height. So that's why he created his voice that had the power. It had that beef behind it. There were some great performances though, don't get me wrong. There were some really nice performances.

One criticism was there was too much heavy rock, do you agree with that?

No, because Freddie liked rock. That was what he did. These were the artists that wanted to be there and the performances that they gave were memorable. My job at that concert was to take the singers to the stage and back. Until Elizabeth Taylor arrived and then I had to look after her.

The other day I had a phone call from my nephew who is ten years old and my niece who is eight. They started singing 'Bohemian Rhapsody' and 'Don't Stop Me Now' down the phone to me. My nephew is Queen and Freddie mad at the moment. He goes on YouTube and watches all the videos. Why do you think Freddie's music still connects so much with young people?

Well, what I do here, there's two of us, we go around schools, talking to kids of thirteen years old upwards, doing HIV/AIDS seminars. You know, making them aware. ALL of these kids know of Freddie Mercury. Why does the music connect with them? It's good! It's good music! We still listen to Chopin, we listen to Bach, we listen to Beethoven.

They wrote good music. Freddie wrote good music. Whilst it might seem complicated, whilst it might seem difficult, he wrote music that people could hum along to and remember. They're listening to, every weekend, 'We are the Champions'. That was written how many years ago? Forty-something years ago…?

Yes, 1977.

They are still singing it. Young kids, even younger than thirteen-year-olds, they're singing it. Perhaps they don't know who wrote it but I'm sure in time they will. Freddie wrote great music!

Peter Freestone was speaking to David Geldard.

Live Killers

Queen's official biographer on his Top 5 Queen Gigs

Jim Jenkins with David Geldard

#5. Elland Road Stadium, Leeds, 1982 (Hot Space Tour)

The reason I picked this one is that I personally think it is one of THE best shows that Queen ever performed. In a way I wish that had been filmed instead of the Milton Keynes gig on that Tour, as good as Milton Keynes was, especially 'Somebody to Love' (which is probably the best live version I've heard). I have to say though, the atmosphere in Leeds was just exhilarating!

It was open air, we had hot weather. I remember taking my shirt off, it was that hot. The band gave 100% and I just loved it. I loved the Hot Space Tour, believe it or not. I actually heard the songs from 'Hot Space' live before the record came out, because the first shows in Europe were before the album was released. So I knew 'Action This Day', 'Staying Power', and 'Back Chat' from a live situation. Of course, when it came to the Leeds gig, I'd heard the album. I'd got the album and the album versions were totally different to the versions they were playing live. I remember being a little bit disappointed with the album versions (at first). I mean, 'Action This Day' was rock-y at the gigs but on the album, it was a bit different, with the synthesisers. Over the years, I've grown to like those tracks very, very much. I love 'Hot Space', it's great. It's great summer-weather listening.

I agree! I always think it was similar to what Michael Jackson was trying to do at the time, which was trying to meld together disco and rock.

Yes! With 'Beat It', for example… Yes, both of them went through the same thing, didn't they? Maybe that was the influence of Freddie working with Michael? I don't know, maybe they took something from each other? I like the experimental way they went about things but Queen live were a totally different kettle of fish to Queen on record. On record you've got the multi-layered harmonies and they were wearing the tape out… Whereas live, it was very, very different. Also, they had a keyboard player on the tour, Morgan Fisher, so that added something a little bit different. I remember Freddie standing up on one of the catwalks, standing up tall, like a peacock, proud, and I could hear keyboards and I thought, "Eh? What's that?! Freddie's not at the piano!". So that added something to it. So, for me, the Leeds gig just worked. As I say, the weather helped. It was just a great gig for the atmosphere, it was electrifying! It stands out for me. I really do think it was one of their best gigs and I think Brian May has stated that in an interview. For anyone who was there, they will remember it, it was a brilliant, brilliant day.

Because of the age that I was in 1982 (eight years old), I didn't hear any of the Hot Space Tour until 1987 or 88. I bought a bootleg VHS from a record fair, of the Channel 4 broadcast of the Milton Keynes gig for 'The Tube'. Then, strangely enough, the first time I heard the Leeds gig was on another bootleg and someone had put it on the coach stereo, when we were travelling down to 'The Freddie Mercury Tribute' at Wembley in 1992. You can tell in that recording, that Queen were just really up for it, there is a special atmosphere to it.

Yes, it was one of the most special atmospheres I've ever experienced at a gig. I don't know why. Maybe because there were loads of Scousers there, a load of people from Manchester, loads from Yorkshire obviously. Put them all together and it was an audience that any band would die for. Honestly, if you can hear that on a tape, can you imagine what it was like there?

This, for me, relates to a bit of a cliché that I always have an issue with. A few people always try to say that Queen were a bit down on their luck before Live Aid and I just think that's nonsense. They were playing huge stadiums on The Hot Space Tour and a few months before Live Aid, they headlined Rock in Rio before 250,000 people.

Actually, I read that a couple of days ago. I thought, "that's a load of crap!". They'd done the big South American Stadiums in 1981 and broke world records, that was the year before Leeds. Also, remember, they did two nights in Rio at the beginning of 1985.

Live Aid, for me, showed the rest of the world what I had been going on about for more than ten years, it just proved it. I remember the Liverpool Echo headline on the Monday night, I think it was "Wembley Wonders". I wasn't shocked, I don't think any Queen fan was shocked about Live Aid. I remember one of the guys saying to me on the Monday, "Was it all the Queen Fan Club in the audience?" and I went, "No, not at all". It just showed how good they were. It was Freddie, let's be honest. Freddie was the master and he just worked everybody up. When he come walking out with his "Daaay-oooh!" he got them all going. And then starting with 'Bohemian Rhapsody' was just…

Genius!

Yes, it was! That was pure genius! They showed the world what we all knew and had done for years.

#4. Hammersmith Odeon, London, 26 December 1979 (Crazy Tour)

The last night of the Crazy Tour, oh my, what a gig! The Crazy Tour was a fantastic tour. My favourite tour, not just of Queen but any band. I did loads of gigs on that tour and every one of them was standout. The Hammersmith Odeon gig was on Boxing Day. I never thought I'd by travelling to London on a Boxing Day. They gave up their time for Boxing Day and the crew did too. It was the last night of the tour and the crew, probably from around the world, didn't go home for Christmas because they had this last gig to do.

From the minute the lights went out, that place erupted. The Hammersmith Odeon, I'd seen quite a few gigs over the years there by different people, but again, it was the atmosphere. The band were just on fire and what I love about that gig, it was their last gig of the seventies and it was the last gig that Queen played in their early days. They changed after that gig because on the next tour they were playing those huge indoor stadiums in America due to the success of 'The Game' album. So, Hammersmith Odeon, it was Christmas and the band had a little bit of fun. Freddie was quite playful. I remember Brian played 'Silent Night' in his guitar solo, that stands out. It was absolutely faultless. I remember a couple of bulbs going out on the lighting rig.

Talking of the lighting rig, I think that lighting rig is the one that the band christened the Pizza Oven, was the best lighting rig I've ever seen at any concert. It was very special, especially when it was tilted at the beginning of the show and they hit the stage with the opening thunder, dry ice, flashing lights and the rig lifted up throughout the concert. At the very end it tilted back and all the red and green lights all became white, joining the white lights for 'God Save The Queen' at the end of the show. My God, the heat! I was at the front on most of the nights of that tour and the lights were burning my face! So, I don't know what it must have been doing to the band on the stage.

I felt they excelled on that tour. 'Crazy Little Thing Called Love' was high in the charts, it was doing really well in the U.K. and I think after a couple of years of not having them in theatres, I think people liked having them back in a theatre and that never happened again. So, Hammersmith '79 was the last theatre show, the last show of the 70s and there was an image change after that and a sound change as well. All the songs they performed just rocked, it was a very, very special gig for me.

My Mum, my sister and my friends went. One of my friends, Mike, it was his birthday at the gig and Freddie passed him a bottle of Champagne for his birthday. We were talking to them on the stage, it was quite funny, "Tie your shoelace John!". At the end of 'Crazy Little Thing Called Love' we carried on clapping, singing and got the band to do a reprise.

This is another one… I was too young. I was at infant school when this happened…

Thank you for making me feel old! *[laughs]*

It's another one that I could only ever hear because of bootlegs and you mention that performance of 'Crazy Little Thing Called Love', and that is my favourite part of that concert. The band finish the song and the fans carry it on for ages until the band come in again.

Yes, once Roger started again on the drum, we knew we'd got them [laughs]. You've got my head buzzing now with memories!

That gig was pro-shot too wasn't it? I'd love to see that come out as an official release.

I do know that Queen Productions have the film of that gig but they haven't got the audio master tapes. Which is a shame because you can't link those together for Blu-ray for today's technology. I think the audio must have gone missing. They did a compilation TV show because although it was the last night of their tour, it was actually a charity gig.

It was for Kampuchea, wasn't it?

Yes, that's right, Kampuchea, Cambodia, and they made a compilation TV special of all the clips of all the other bands. There was a lot of other bands like Wings who followed but Queen did a full show of their own, the rest was like a tribute concert where all different people pile on stage. So, they made a television show and I think the sound master tapes probably went off to use for the television, they used 'Now I'm Here' and 'Crazy Little Thing'. It's sad that they haven't got that audio because it's fantastic isn't it? I would be great to have that on a DVD/Blu-ray/CD release.

I remember at the end of the show, outside, Peter Straker coming out and my Mum shouting to him "Commander!" because he had just played the Commander in 'Doctor Who' and she recognised him! So that's my number four gig and The Crazy Tour was my favourite tour of my life. It was absolutely fantastic. Probably the best month of my life, if I'm being honest.

#3. Pavilion de Paris, Paris, France, 1 March 1979 (Jazz Tour)

I had to go for Paris! The Live Killers/Jazz Tour. We went to the very last three nights of that tour, which were in Paris. It was strange seeing them for three consecutive nights, which were built up. So, on the first night it was like, "Wow!" and the second night they were just better than the first night. On third night, a bit like Leeds, I would put that as one of the best gigs of their career. It happened to be the longest gig that Queen ever played. The good news is that Queen Productions has got the film, the master audio tapes and you know that on the 'Bohemian Rhapsody' film soundtrack, you hear 'Fat Bottomed Girls'? The track on that album shows you what the show was like. It was brilliant! We travelled over from the UK and a friend joined us from Dublin as well. Back then, you didn't do that. It's very common today, to go to Europe or to go to wherever to see a concert. But, you know, in 1979, it wasn't something that was really done. We did it and the band were quite amused, I think, having British fans at the Paris show. I think we upset a few of the French fans because Freddie said he wanted to hear some of the French voices, not just the English ones! [laughs]

We were at the front every night. Another special reason that I chose the Paris gig as well, the band performed 'Bicycle Race', which was a single. They performed it at the show and we all decided to take bicycle bells with us. We kept them quiet and then when they started 'Bicycle Race', we all rang them. Then, on the second night, a load of French fans had been out and bought bicycle bells! So, by the third night, I don't think any shop in Paris had any bicycle bells left. I think everyone in there took a bicycle bell with them. Of course, on the second night, Freddie actually said, "Good Evening, have you brought your bicycle bells tonight?". Before the show, we asked one of the roadies, Chris 'Crystal' Taylor, "Would Freddie ring the bell?". He was like, "Hmmm…ok, I'll ask him, if he says no, no deal." But he did. So, on that last night they played 'Bicycle Race' and instead of going right in to 'I'm In Love with My Car', it stopped. Freddie got up from the piano and walked over to us all with his bicycle bell, rang the bell and said to us all, "You're mad!". He then went back to the piano and on with the show. That was a very, very special moment during the gig.

There were quite few of you, hardcore fans who travelled to all the gigs, who were christened The Royal Family. How many of you were in that group?

Yes, well that was where that all kicked off from. There was about thirty of us in Paris, I think. No more than thirty. Then they did a show in the summer, in Germany, in Saarbrücken, and we all decided to go to that as well. Then there was The Crazy Tour and we did ALL the shows on The Crazy Tour too. We were making a spectacle of ourselves and Freddie found it quite amusing.

Then in an interview Freddie said, "We have our very own Royal Family" and that stuck. That's how we got the name. We were just fans who travelled around watching the band, the next minute, we're known as The Royal Family. The fans, still to this day, refer to us all as The Royal Family, which is really nice.

#2. Empire Theatre, Liverpool, 1 November, 1974 (Sheer Heart Attack Tour).

I had to pick that one. I was going to go for the Rainbow Theatre gig. The reason I went for the Liverpool show was because I realised at that show that they were really going to be mega. I had been to many shows at the Liverpool Empire and I hadn't witnessed anything like that show. If you think about it, they'd only had one hit single, with 'Seven Seas of Rhye'. 'Killer Queen/Flick of the Wrist' was on the way up in the charts. 'Sheer Heart Attack' hadn't been released. I remember the lights going out and it was just bedlam. Honestly, it went wild. They actually dropped the safety curtain. It came down and the manager, Mr. O'Neill his name was, walked on stage with his dinner suit on and the lights came back on. He went' "Calm down! Will you just go back to your seats?" because people rushed the stage. He said, "The show is not going to start until you all move back! Move back!". Then the next thing is the 'Procession' tape started [laughs]. The place just went bonkers! Of course, Charlie O' Neill left the stage, the lights went out, the safety curtain rose back up and they came on stage. I'd never witnessed anything like that. If I had to pick up one moment of the gig, it's going to be that one. They opened with a song that we didn't know: 'Now I'm Here'. The album hadn't been released, so we didn't know the song.

The place was in darkness. We heard [imitates the guitar riff]... "Here I stand…" and Freddie sang "Now I'm Here" and appeared on the left-hand side of the stage. The place just erupted. There was more noise than when the lights went out. "Now I'm there…" and Freddie appeared on the right! "I'm just a…" and the stage lights came on and Freddie was standing in the middle of the stage with his winged Zhandra Rhodes top on. You could feel the place was dancing. I have never witnessed anything like it at the Empire since then. It's very different today. It was such a fantastic gig. We were getting new songs that we didn't know. They played my favourite Queen song ever, 'March of the Black Queen'.

I love that song!

Then you had the delicate tones of 'White Queen'. Freddie said "We're going to play you a song" and it was another song from 'Queen II' because they'd done a couple, 'Father to Son' and 'Ogre Battle'. So, they did 'White Queen' and it was just unbelievable. The audience were so respectful. At the end of the roar I remember Freddie saying, "You do like 'Queen II'!" and we were like, "We LOVE 'Queen II'!". Like I said, we got the new songs off 'Sheer Heart Attack'. I remember 'Stone Cold Crazy'. That was so punky! Punk music wasn't even out then, was it? It really rocked. It was an exciting show. I remember all the dry ice during 'In the Lap of the Gods (Revisited)'. We got 'Big Spender', which always went down really well. I went for Liverpool Empire because I had to have a Liverpool gig. Queen were very popular in London, and obviously in Cornwall, Roger Taylor's home territory. The band then said, "We're getting a following now in Liverpool". They'd played here a couple of times with Mott the Hoople and a couple of shows on their own. That gig, on 1 November, was the third night of the tour. They'd done Manchester, and they'd done Hanley, in Stoke-on-Trent the night before Liverpool. It must have blown them away. The reaction of the crowd, they were so welcoming. They'd been around a long time. It was the year after the Mott the Hoople tour and they'd gone down really well on that. So, I had to pick a hometown gig and of every tour I've been to and every gig, that would probably be my number one. I just thought, they were so hungry. They excelled with their playing. During 'White Queen' you get a section, you'll know it, where they do that instrumental part and you got to see each of them in their own right. Freddie on the piano, John on the bass, Roger thundering away at the back and holding everything together, Brian making sounds like there were loads on stage, not just one.

For me, that song is just absolute perfection.

Isn't it? That was my live number one song ever. I just think it's perfect. The way they perform it is unique. I'll use your word and say, genius, because it really is, live. So that tour, the '74 tour, proved to me with what I was witnessing, they were going to be big! Look where they went after that…

That tour seems like it was a real defining moment for Queen. This seems like the moment they went 'nuclear'.

It did! It was like a volcano erupting! I'd never witnessed anything like that, I've never seen anything like that since. There are some great bands out there, I'm not going to name them but they are extremely special and, live, they excel. But that gig, 1 November 1974, stands out for me and that's why I picked it. I knew, "This band is going to be huge!" and I was right [laughs].

#1. Hyde Park, London, 18 September 1976 (Free Summer concert).

Jim, what was is about this concert that makes it your number one choice?

It's a combination. I had tickets to see them in Edinburgh, two nights in Edinburgh, and they changed the date of the gigs and I was going away on 27 August. They changed the date of the gigs to after that, I wasn't here and I was going to miss them. I'll tell you, having to send tickets back because I couldn't go made me feel sick. Then they added Cardiff and I thought "They're playing Edinburgh and Cardiff, surely they're going to play Belfast and London?", because they were calling it a UK mini tour. They didn't add Belfast, which was a shame really because they never played Belfast, ever. Then, on the day before I was going away, I got a phone call from the fan club secretary and she said to me, "They've added London. What date do you get back from your holiday? I said "I get back on 17 September". So, she said, "They're playing Hyde Park on the 18th". I said, "Right, I want a ticket!", she said, "There's no tickets – it's free, they're doing a free concert". "What? I haven't got to pay for it?", not that the tickets were dear, they were only like £4 or something [about £25 in today's money], probably not even that. So, it was a combination of, I'd just got back from holiday, I'd missed three shows on the tour, I was getting to see them, it was free, I'd never not paid for a concert before and it was the crowd! I had never, ever been in a crowd of that number of people before.

They were saying there were in between 150,000 to 250,000 people there.

I was so tired, I was jetlagged. I remember Steve Hillage being on stage and I just slept. I remember Kiki Dee. I remember one of the audience thought he was Jesus, he was on about the Second Coming and kept walking around us. He was trying to wake me up and give me some extra strength to stay awake. I couldn't wait for Queen to come on and, boy, when they came on, the place erupted! Of course, they opened with a song that was the biggest, 'Bohemian Rhapsody'. It just got the crowd in the mood, didn't it? During the show they played a brand-new song, it was just Freddie alone at the piano, I'd never seen that before at a Queen gig. Just Fred, on his own, just tinkling away, singing this ballad called 'You Take My Breath Away'.

He told us all to be quiet at the start and [laughs] and everybody did! The power of that man was incredible. So, we all shut up and were silent to listen to the song. The gig was amazing, the weather again was really warm, it was a fantastic outdoor gig. The sad thing was, they were due to come back on and do an encore and they were going to finish with another brand-new song, 'Tie Your Mother Down', which they had performed in Edinburgh and Cardiff. But the police wouldn't let them go back on stage, because of the crowd of people, they were worried about people leaving the park and heading out onto the streets of London. They went and switched all the lights off! So, they turned the band's power off on the stage and they turned all the lights off outdoors as well. So, we all left that park in darkness. I remember friends coming down from Liverpool who I actually went and met. Me and my mates had been there since 5 o'clock at the front and then I went to meet my friends from Liverpool. I was staying down in London that night and I remember leaving the park, on the Underground and my friends going back to Euston to get the late-night train back.

That was a really special show. I don't think it was the best performance Queen ever gave, but the atmosphere of the crowd and what the band did give, makes it stand out. It was just my favourite gig ever.

Looking at the setlist for that gig, Jim, it was just incredible. It's like the best of the early years.

Yes! Four albums' worth, wasn't it? I feel with the Hyde Park gig, it was the end of the beginning. In 1977, you'll know, they played provincial theatres in the U.K., they were different. It was a different scale. It was the production, with the moving crown lighting rig, Earls Court, there was a change in the band in those 1977 shows. So, Hyde Park was the end of the very beginning of those early shows and they did it as a thank you for the success of 'Bohemian Rhapsody' and 'A Night at the Opera'. It was very memorable and a very stressful gig, it's in my heart. That's why it's number one.

That's an awesome Top 5 Jim! Now, let's talk about Queen's final concert, at Knebworth Park in 1986. In the public's mind, The Magic Tour is Queen live, I think.

Yes, you know why? It's the yellow jacket. Seriously, I think people remember that tour because of the clothes, the T-shirts, John Deacon's Hilda Ogden T-shirt! For some reason they remember it for the clothes, that sounds odd but that image of Freddie with the yellow jacket, I think people remember that. I don't think people realised that was the end, no more. It ended at Knebworth. Freddie looked very relaxed at Knebworth. At the end of the show didn't John Deacon throw his bass?

Yes, he did.

I was like, "What was that about? It wasn't a bad gig?" They didn't play bad; the crowd was fantastically up for it. The band were up for it. Why has he gone and done that? Sometimes I think, "Did he realise then?". That was it. He'd never play with Queen again. I don't know. Knebworth was a good gig but it's tinged with sadness now, it was the last time I ever saw Queen.

Did you prefer Knebworth to Wembley?

That's an interesting question. I don't know. Maybe? You see the thing is with The Magic Tour , I felt the best one was at Newcastle, St. James' Park. That was the best one of the tour, that was before Wembley. Freddie was really relaxed and the band played really well at Knebworth, so maybe. Maybe it was better than Wembley, yes.

Moving on to 1992: this was the first time I saw any of the Queen members live, at The Freddie Mercury Tribute Concert. What are your memories?

Easter Monday. I organised a coach from Liverpool to take people down to Wembley. The coach stopped right outside the steps, where you walk up. We all got off the bus and walked up, not realising there was a queue and we just walked straight in! That was quite funny.

They were giving us red ribbons and I'd spent weeks and weeks here, in the house, making them with friends. I remember we were very drunk and everyone was getting pins stuck in their body. Anyway, that's another story [laughs].

I remember we walked straight onto the pitch, and everybody ran to get down to the front and I thought, "No. I don't want to go down to the front". A couple of us decided to go and sit in front of the mixing desk and that's where I stayed all day. I didn't go backstage; I had a pass to go backstage but I didn't go. I stayed with my friends on the pitch and watched excellent musicians performing.

You're not going to believe this but I can't tell you much about it. I remember George Michael singing 'Somebody To Love'. I remember Extreme, Gary Cherone singing tons. I remember Joe Elliott and Roger Daltrey. The rest of it… I was so upset. Because I could see three members of Queen and one of them wasn't there. I remember Freddie coming up on the screen and I remember bursting into tears. That was the end of the show for me. I remember that one of my mates I was with, he doesn't cry, I remember he looked up into the sky and there was one shining star. It was really strange and he said, "Look, Freddie's looking down on us!". We burst into tears and so did everyone around us.

I remember Liza Minnelli coming on and I thought, "Oh my God!", I nearly had a heart attack with her singing Freddie's song because he idolised her. I remember her singing 'We are the Champions' and saying, "Freddie, just to let you know we were thinking of you!". The next thing, we were in a service station on the way home, buying all the newspapers, I can't even remember leaving the stadium. It's like a haze in my mind, that gig. I get flashes of it, it's very strange.

My Mum was there. I got a ticket in the Royal Box, which I gave to my sister. So my sister sat in the Royal Box with my Mum, I was on the pitch with all my friends. That's where I wanted to be to watch that show. It's funny because when I watch it on the telly, I've got no memory. It's like I wasn't there. I was so upset. I think my emotions took over me that day. I do remember seeing Billy Squier on stage. I was like, "Wow! Why didn't he sing?".

Yes, The Scorpions came on at the end too!

I didn't see them; I can't remember that. My memory of that gig, and this is not a gripe because it was it was a rock gig and it went down great, didn't it? I felt Liza Minnelli showed Freddie. It was him. And that's what the show lacked, for me personally. Where was Erasure? Where was Culture Club, Spandau Ballet? People like that, that Freddie loved. You're going to laugh… I even expected The Andrews Sisters. I know it sounds ridiculous. I didn't know who was going to be on, I didn't want to know. I was saying, "Don't tell me who'll be on, it'll be a surprise" and of course you got to know on the way down to Wembley on the coach because they were all taking about it, it was in the papers. Everyone was going on about George Michael being on. I was like, "Wham? What the heck… He's good but… George Michael doing Queen songs?". Of course, on the way back it was, "Wasn't George Michael fantastic!" That's what I remember of the gig.

Here's a memory, I'd forgotten and it's just come to me. People around me were looking at their watches because they'd set the timer on the video recorder at home.

I did the same, well, my Mum taped it for me.

I remember when George Michael finished, everyone was saying, "It's going to switch off now!" It was Easter Monday, 20 April. I didn't get home until 5am on the Tuesday. I was knackered. Then of course we were watching the recording. I remember going to work…

You're kidding?

No, I went to work on the Tuesday morning but I had to come home. I came home in the afternoon and went to bed, until Wednesday morning.

When we left the Wembley Stadium, we saw Spinal Tap getting into their limo and they gave us a wave. Then we all got on the coach and my mate thought he saw David Bowie. So, he got off the bus and tried to get his autograph. I think we ended up being one of the last coaches there. I don't think we arrived back in Stockport until 7am.

Oh my God! I can't remember leaving the stadium. Isn't that strange? I wasn't drunk, I didn't have a drink at all. I was just emotionally wrecked.

Have you got a favourite solo gig by a Queen member?

It would be Roger Taylor. Probably The Cross if I'm honest. I loved The Cross. I'll go for Hammersmith Palais. It was a Queen Fan Club Christmas party [4 December 1988]. The Cross played and they were absolutely amazing. Roger brought Brian and John on stage. They did 'Let Me Out' from the 'Starfleet' mini-album. I'm also thinking of The Cross on 'Meltdown', you know the television show? I went to that recording. 6 November 1987. But I'll go for The Cross at Hammersmith Palais. If you count that as solo.

If I had to pick a proper solo gig, I'd go for Roger Taylor at Liverpool L2 [27 March 1999]. Just for 'Tenement Funster'. To hear 'Tenement Funster' live was one of the highlights because I love that song and I still think it sounds great on 'Sheer Heart Attack'.

It's funny that you remember my mates and I, singing in the bar, at Roger's Manchester University gig in 1999, decades before we became friends.

I do remember that! Everyone was singing! It was the John Deacon Fan Club! [A group of fans in the late 90s who would go to gigs dressed as John Deacon]

We started it! Because we'd had a few drinks. We saw the John Deacon Fan Club and we started singing 'Dragon Attack' to them and playing air bass!

Yes, they started singing their heads off and everyone joined in! I can remember that, it was fun.

In the end we got asked to leave...

You did, because you were noisy and they told you to shut up! The fella behind the bar got narked. I don't know why; you weren't doing any harm. I remember we actually did that at the convention that year and that was after that gig. So, yes, I do remember that, everyone singing and stamping their feet to 'Dragon Attack'.

Over The Rainbow

Martin Green

Once upon a time when everything closed on Sundays, my parents would take us window shopping at Hamleys. One of my vivid 1970s childhood memories happened then, not at the world's greatest toy shop, but around the corner on Carnaby Street. I can clearly recall staring lovingly at a pair of multicoloured striped glitter platform shoes displayed in one of the boutiques. I'd only seen such thrilling footwear on 'Top Of The Pops', but this was real life. This wasn't fantasy.

As we lived in East London, dad had a choice of two routes when driving his silver Ford Capri into the West End. I always hoped he would travel along the A503. Why? Because that journey took us directly past a place that, aside from Disneyland, I dreamed of visiting. A magical landmark called The Rainbow.

Being a pop-obsessed 70s kid, I proudly wore my Slade T-Shirt, devoured 'Look-In' magazine, glued myself to LWT's 'Supersonic' and blasted out '48 Crash' by Suzi Quatro, the first single I ever bought. I was nuts about that record, although couldn't understand why my mother told me not to play the B-side. She didn't think a song titled 'Little Bitch Blue' was appropriate for my seven-year-old ears. I may not have known about the meaning of those provocative female rock lyrics, but I certainly knew about The Rainbow.

Built as a cinema in 1930, the vast space had been designed in a Hollywood Moorish style with a Mediterranean village perched high above the auditorium. Soon after re-opening as a rock venue in 1971, this Art Deco escapist fantasia with its trickling foyer fountain and twinkling celestial ceiling became immensely popular and quickly gained fame after being featured on news reports about hordes of emotional teens queuing to see The Osmonds, Sweet and T.Rex. The Rainbow's robust red logo emblazoned across the front of the building filled my teenybopper mind with excitement. I yearned to be inside there every time we drove by. A few years later my pop prayers were answered.

The first Queen album I ever heard was 'A Night At The Opera', which I borrowed from a mate's older rocker brother. It was 1976 and I'd already bought 'Bohemian Rhapsody', which debuted on our brand new Ferguson Music Centre. My best pal Alan Sparkes lived nearby and we used to lie on the living room floor and position the record player speakers either side of our heads in order to fully experience the extreme stereo panning on 'The Prophet's Song'. Our young minds were blown as we listened to the wise man.

At that time new LPs were expensive, so we used to borrow each other's and occasionally swap. Alan had 'News of The World' and the following year I received 'Jazz' as a Christmas present. Being such big Queen fans we asked if we could paint the band's logo on the bonnet of Alan's Dad's old Rover. But he fiercely objected. We couldn't understand why. He liked them too. Was he in love with his car? My mother soon explained that Mr Sparkes, who was a big, burly, mechanic, didn't want Queen sprayed on his motor as the word also meant homosexual. We never asked again.

In 1979 the band released 'Crazy Little Thing Called Love' and announced a UK tour. Alan's dad agreed to take us. I was 13 and going to see my first ever gig, plus it was happening at The Rainbow. I was ecstatic. On 14 December we watched the lights go down and an enormous multi-coloured lighting rig rise from the darkened stage, propelling us directly into the cover of 'Live Killers'. The excitement was incredible. Freddie burst onto the stage with surprisingly short hair and tight bright red leather trousers, firmly shaking off the sheer 70s and propelling himself into the homoerotic 80s.

The Crazy Tour set was a full-on, non-stop thrill ride, and they only disappeared during the complicated operatic section of 'Bohemian Rhapsody', which I presume was played from a reel-to-reel tape. The band exploded back on to the stage and, although we didn't realise it, this would be the last time Queen would play such intimate venues. We were extraordinarily lucky.

Around the same time, I had been seduced by my aunt's copy of 'Ziggy Stardust' and within months became obsessed with Bowie, who took my hand and guided me towards Lou Reed, The Velvets, Kraftwerk, Brian Eno, Roxy Music, The Human League and Talking Heads.

As the 1980s dawned I turned my back on '70s rock, swapping my shiny Yes transfer T-Shirt for a Street Theatre pirate shirt and my Adidas trainers for a pair of grey leather Tukka boots. I was soon going to see Soft Cell, Depeche Mode, B-52s, Birthday Party, and Bauhaus. I plugged in my crimpers and unplugged Queen. I never mentioned seeing them to my new cool art school friends.

Ten years later in 1991, while House music dominated London's nightlife, I co-founded 'Smashing', where I could DJ anything I wanted, mixing up Bowie, Bacharach, Beastie Boys, Bolan and The Beatles. Soon our eclectic weekly club attracted other outsiders, misfits and mis-shapes including Pulp, Blur, Leigh Bowery, Pam Hogg, Peter Doig, Elastica, Denim and indie kids in bands soon to be labelled 'Britpop'.

'Smashing' was described by Dave Swindells at 'Time Out' as "a party in your bedroom" and each week I would dig through the dark depths of my record boxes to find forgotten gems. This was in the days before Spotify, when you really had to get your hands dirty. One night in 1993 I dug out my old copy of 'Jazz' and played 'Don't Stop Me Now'. The illuminated dance floor erupted as the crowd went crazy, zooming around like rocket ships with arms outstretched. They were having a good time and didn't want to stop at all. That night I fell in love with Queen all over again.

Nowadays, I proudly announce on any given opportunity that Queen were the first band I ever saw live. It impresses everyone. Even though I didn't listen to them for a decade, I still kept the souvenir programme from that magical night at the legendary Rainbow. Ironically the venue where we once worshipped rock gods is now an alternative place of praise, having become an evangelical church. Queen continue to uplift our spirits and Freddie Mercury is certainly in Heaven entertaining the flock of angels.

First loves never die. They remain with you forever.

Missed Opportunities

Teo Torriatte

This is not your typical account of "What happened to me in a Queen-related scenario..". This is, in fact, the story of quite a few missed experiences.

I always had a slight penchant for Brian. I remember watching the 'I Want it All' video when I was about thirteen and being over-jealous of his hair. I even got a perm trying to imitate it – spoiler: It didn't work! - but then, I've always tended to favour guitarists in rock bands.

My teenage years were marked by Brian's first solo record, although I actually never bought it until a quarter of century later. But I spent hours dancing to 'Driven By You' and listening to 'Too Much Love Will Kill You'. Whenever those songs came on the radio, I'd tape them on cassette – that was the Spotify of my generation.

And then the Brian May Band came to Barcelona for a concert. If there is a concert I still regret to not have attended, it's that one. Not the Magic Tour, or Freddie's appearance in Montjuïc. The 1993 Brian concert. I almost went. I knew plenty of people who did. I could have joined them. But I was an atypical teenager, too frightened of enjoying myself. I know this sounds strange, but it took me many years to take care of my mental health and, as a result, missed out many experiences like concerts, holidays, nights out…

Same happened with the Another World tour a handful of years later. Same exact situation: never joined those who went because I felt I was not worthy of enjoying the pleasures of life. I wasn't a teenager anymore by then, but I had still not overcome my demons.

Fast forward to 2018. I was a middle-aged woman, with a relatively stable and mildly comfortable life, and although I still suffered from anxiety on a regular basis, I had managed to enjoy life and being happy in a quite realistic way. I had travelled, I had gone to concerts, I had enjoyed many experiences that I should have done years earlier.

June 2018: Queen and Adam Lambert were visiting Barcelona. I hesitated about buying a ticket but in the end, I opted to buy one for the Ringo Starr concert the week after. At the time some family problems were keeping me busy, and I didn't want to risk losing the money of two tickets if I finally couldn't attend, plus the anxiety of not knowing my real availability until the last minute. Again, I regret my choice. The Ringo Starr concert was fine, but nowhere the fun I'd have had on the Q+AL one. Those who went testified it for me. However, at the time I was still a fan who mostly knew only about the 'Greatest Hits'.

November 2018: The 'Bohemian Rhapsody' film came out and I went to watch it on cinema. I was absolutely speechless. I went back to watch it again the day after. I watched it more than thirty times in cinemas, and, in the meantime, I went into a fanatic Queen shopping spree, and got the full discography, plus solo works and other stuff, like Brian's 3D books. I discovered so many songs that I love that I had never heard before. I've never played 'Greatest Hits' again.

I've even found the perfect song for treating my anxiety: 'She Makes Me (Stormtrooper in Stilettos)' has been of great help to me whenever I need to breath.

Another missed chance – but this time it wasn't my, or anyone's, fault – was on 22 December 2018. We went to Carnaby Street just for the day – take a plane at 6.00 am, come back in the evening – to visit Queen's store and see the Bohemian Rhapsody Christmas lights. On the train, on the way back to the airport in the evening, I saw an Instagram post by Brian, on the very same street that rainy afternoon, with his son Jimmy. We had probably missed him by a few minutes. I felt totally unlucky, although if I had actually bumped into him, I'd probably had been unable to react anyway.

I am lucky enough to have interacted with Brian on Instagram. He has liked a few of my comments so far, but the day he actually replied to one, my heart was almost going out of my chest. Who knew that such a simple action could bring such emotions to a fan?

Then the announcement for a European Tour came. First, I bought tickets for Amsterdam and couldn't be more excited when the dates for Madrid were added. Bought tickets for there too, the most expensive I could afford. I was counting the days, literally. Sadly, the pandemic came, and then the re-scheduled dates for 2021 had also to be postponed. I still held my tickets for 2022, I really couldn't bear the thought of missing them again. I felt it would not have been fair.

I have also started guitar lessons and I bought my very own Red Special from his shop. Although I am a slow learner, I really enjoy the process. I am lucky to have a very patient teacher and I somehow feel I am no more that person who used to think "it's not worth trying, you are not going to manage". Now, I am more a "who cares what others think?" type of person.

To try to comfort myself over the pandemic times, I got a 'Back To The Light' tattoo recently – I got a '39 one on December 2018, too. I feel like going back to my younger years and trying to reconcile with that silly girl who was so lost in life, to tell her that in the end, everything was going to be all right. By doing this, I feel the circle is somehow completed. Thank you, Brian.

Denise Silcock Interview

Queen fan Denise Silcock has hosted several Queen-themed fundraising parties to raise money for AIDS charities in Freddie's name such as 1996's Red Ribbon Making Day for Red Ribbon International.

When did your love of Queen begin?

It was way back... 'Sheer Heart Attack' was the first album I bought. That was the introduction for me. I mean, the cover kept me happy for a while! [laughs] So, it was 1974 and I was at school. I used to carry my 'Sheer Heart Attack' album to school, because we had a room where we could all go and play music. Everybody got sick of me, playing my 'Brighton Rock'! I thought it was marvellous. I loved the inner sleeve with all the lyrics on. Not only that but 'In the Lap Of The Gods'... Roger's voice! My goodness me! That was it for me. My friend Barbara's boyfriend, who had the album first, he said, "Have you heard this band called Queen? They're brilliant". He put the record on and… [imitates Roger's falsetto vocal]… I thought "Oh my God! Who is that?". That was it for me.

To this day, I don't know how he managed to reach those notes.

Oh, I know! Honestly, I was just taken in, hook, line and sinker. That was my band and that was it for me and I wasn't going to change. There was no way. I remember the concert that sticks in my head was the Hammersmith Odeon one at Christmas. It was a live concert from 'The Old Grey Whistle Test', I think it was broadcast on BBC 2. I remember saying to my Mum, "Mum! This is that band! Look at them, look at them! Aren't they brilliant?". She went, "Ooooh! That's a bit unusual!". That always makes me smile because it reminds me of my Mum. But my favourite album is definitely 'Sheer Heart Attack'.

So did you ever get to see them live?

No, which is awful. I've seen Roger a few times, Brian as well and I went to The Freddie Mercury Tribute Concert. But as for Queen, I didn't get a chance, sadly. I would have loved to have seen them live but out of my collection of videos and things like that, my collection of concerts and stuff... there's one in particular, 'Queen Live in Paris' 1979. It's absolutely tremendous. It was one that we picked up in a little shop in Manchester, back in the days of the Corn Exchange and Affleck's Palace where all the record collectors used to be.

I remember it well because I was one of them!

Yes, that used to be 'a thing'. Back then, when we were doing the parties, myself and my friend Carole used to scour the shops every Saturday, looking for new stuff. There was no internet, it was just a case of "get what you can" in that way. It was about finding that little gem. So, this video, the colour has gone on it because it was a copy of a copy of a copy, etc. It's a superb concert.

So what was the story behind the Queen-themed fundraising tribute nights that you put on?

When we lost Freddie, it felt like the world had ended. It was an awful, awful thing. I remember my sister ringing up and asking, "Are you alright love?" because it was like I'd lost a relative. I'd just always been a massive, massive fan. Everything they did, I knew about it or bought it or whatever. So, Roger and Brian did the presentation on the BRIT Awards [1992] and Roger said, "We hope

Denise Silcock and friends, raising funds for Red Ribbon International, Red Ribbon Making Day, 1996. [Photo © D. Silcock.]

that a lot of you will be able to join us on April the 20th at Wembley Stadium for a celebration of Freddie's life and career, a lot of friends are coming and you're all welcome. Please join us!". So, I was like, "That includes us! Off we go, we're going to Wembley!".

I was exactly the same. I was watching that live and I jumped off my seat. I was jumping around the living room, going mad! "I've got to get a ticket!"

Honestly, I couldn't believe it. I even got in touch with my bank manager and asked for an overdraft to get the tickets! He said, "I think you better come in and see us". So I went in and said, "Please, please!", he said, "It's alright, you've got it!" [laughs] I think it was £100 and I thought it was amazing that we'd got enough money for tickets. So, we went to the concert and I remember being on the coach and if you were there you would have got your red ribbon?

Yes I did.

So, when I got back home I thought, "I've got to do something, I can't let this go". I was in a fortunate position where I worked for a newspaper, so I could get into places where other people couldn't. I was ringing around other people. I found a venue, which was only across the road from where I worked. I went and asked them, "Would you mind if we put on a big event? We'll be raising money for AIDS Awareness". They went, "Yes, that's alright!". At the time, there was a lot of stigma went with it as well. So that's how it kicked off. The first one was in April 1993, to celebrate the first anniversary of The Freddie Mercury Tribute Concert. Honest to God, I could not believe the response! It was just incredible, absolutely amazing. We wanted to emulate Freddie's parties, because he was so famous for his parties.

I spoke to the Chef and he was absolutely amazing. He just knew exactly what he wanted. I showed him some videos and things like that. The one thing that he wanted to do was the stack of champagne glasses, and, you know, pour it from the top, but we never actually got around to doing that. But we did do fish in aspic and all that sort of stuff, and we really went to town, doing something that Freddie would have been proud of.

From that first event, there were so many people who became lifelong friends, Carole, Dave, Sharon and loads of other wonderful people we still keep in touch with, nearly thirty years later. Originally, we were just going to do the one event but because people just wanted more and more, we did another one. That was in the September for Freddie's birthday and one in the November, which wasn't a party but a red ribbon-making day. So, you would finish organising one, have a break for a week and start again. We came up with different ideas for the parties, they all had a theme. There was 'Rockin' in Rio' where we had we had a Samba band and stuff like that. It was just, like, thinking outside of the box, if you will.

I remember the 'Seaside Rendevouz' night, where you had a Punch and Judy man, a Brian May tribute act and there was a CD stall. I remember getting a CD that night that had the 'Smile' album on, I was so excited!

That was what it was all about. It was giving people something special. We had people travelling to us from all over the place. It was amazing really.

There was the serious side as well, the AIDS awareness stuff. I was getting invited on to radio shows and talking to politicians about things. I went on training courses for AIDS awareness, just to get more information. That's what I wanted to do as well, make sure that Freddie didn't die in vain and get some important messages across.

We bought a specialist bed for sexual health, that's in Bolton Hospital. We also helped to make one million red ribbons.

That's amazing!

We did loads of things, it was a wonderful time.

There's a funny story. When the 'Made in Heaven' album came out, I was asked to go on BBC Radio Five Live. It was first thing in the morning. They sent a car for me, took me to Manchester and sat me in this little room to link up with London. They played 'Heaven for Everyone' and said "This is from the new album" and it wasn't the right version! It was the 1987 version from Roger's band

The Cross [from the album 'Shove It']. I spotted it right away. I said, "Excuse me, I hope you don't mind me saying but you've got the versions the wrong way round" and they all went, "OH MY GOD!!!". They said can you tell the difference then? I think, basically, they were trying to catch me out. That was one to remember!

I remember you had people from all over the place that came for the parties.

Yes. We had quite a few from Stockport, like you, Jon, Val, etc. We had one lady, when she turned up we'd say, "She's come all the way from Australia" but she was actually on holiday over here! There was a guy called Chris, who was a policeman who used to be outside 10 Downing Street, he used to come to every one, sometimes the ribbon making days as well.

Do you remember when we had Freddie's stamp collection?

Yes, I do!

There was news doing the rounds that Freddie Mercury's stamp collection had been sold. So, I did some digging and ringing around, I was in contact with Queen's press office as well. I used to speak to them and try and get some inside info. I heard they were going to have viewings of the collection. I phoned the stamp museum and spoke to this guy. He hadn't got a clue who Freddie Mercury was, he was a stamp expert. I organised a trip to have a viewing, we had the very first viewing of it as our star prize. So, we visited the Stamp Museum in London, put in a visit to Kensington Market [where Roger and Freddie worked in their pre-fame days] and Freddie's house, Garden Lodge. We did an awful lot of work at the Stamp Museum, because the guy didn't know an awful lot about Freddie Mercury and I did. So, I wrote this big introduction about Freddie and his life in Zanzibar and how it came to be that he had this stamp collection.

We actually had Freddie's stamp collection in our house! When we actually did the viewing of it, it was just incredible. People were just looking at it and bursting into tears.

That was really special. We had some little metal Freddie Mercury busts made and we gave one to the Stamp Museum. Now, the guy who was the curator of this stamp exhibit was travelling all around the world, showing Freddie Mercury's stamp collection and he was using my information, which I thought was wonderful, I was really, really proud of that. In the end, the stamp collection was going to be housed in the museum in London and he told me that he was going to have a display thing made. When I finally got the picture of it, I was like, "Oh my goodness me!". Being such a huge Queen fan, I knew that Freddie said he would like to be buried with his treasures like Tutankhamen, in a pyramid in London.

Can you believe that the stand that they put Freddie's stamp collection in was pyramid shaped? I never even mentioned that. It chills me now.

Now, the question has to be asked Denise, would you ever consider a one-off revival/reunion party?

[Laughs] Well I'd love to but I would look a bit ridiculous now! I certainly couldn't run around in the outfits that I used to wear, I'll tell you that for nothing! [laughs] It would be amazing but it's probably a no. It's best left to memories. Who knows though? Never say never.

I've got to say, that around that time, me and my

mate, Jon Fowler and I were going to lots of those kind of Queen tribute events in Stockport and Greater Manchester. Yours were easily the best. It was obvious that you had put so much thought into it and it is something that we still talk about to this day.

Bless you! Well, we must have done something right. It was just having the love of it. Nowadays, to be perfectly honest, there just aren't the venues anymore, which is a shame. It was special, it was of the moment but if ever Roger said he'd turn up, I'd be there! [laughs]

I remember once, Dave, we used to put out the adverts for the press releases to all the newspapers. One newspaper reported that Brian May was going to attend. You can imagine, my phone was ringing off the wall! People would ring up saying, "I want twenty tickets now!". I was saying, "WHAT?!". They said, "Brian May is going to be there". I said, "No, we have a Brian May tribute act". They replied, "No, Brian May, it says so in the paper!". I had to get in touch with the paper and tell them it was only a tribute, not the real Brian May! It was bonkers.

You mentioned The Freddie Mercury Tribute Concert earlier, what are your memories of that day?

It was the most amazing day ever. Our son, Wayne, was with us he was only about nine or ten years old at the time. We had our yellow jackets that we'd made. Wayne's jacket had a Freddie Mercury logo on the back that we painted on. It was absolutely amazing. I've never cried and laughed so much, it was unbelievable. I got home and I couldn't speak. My voice had gone. We travelled back to Horwich on the coach and when we got home, it was the stupidest thing, we were sat with a bowl of tomato soup and then we watched the video, because we'd taped it. We'd set it to record when we went out and we watched it. I don't know if you remember, but even hearing them checking the equipment ,"One... two... one... two"? That just lit the blue touch paper for me. Just the most incredible day ever.

Any stand out acts for you from that day?

Seeing Roger! [laughs] We were right at the front, more or less. Wayne was only little, he couldn't see anything and it was getting a bit too squashed. So, we asked some of the security people if we could move because it was getting a bit uncomfortable. They moved us forward and we ended up in the seated area, parallel to the stage. When it had all ended, we came down and stood in front of the stage, it was just a few people milling around. This guy came out from the back of the stage and he started throwing Roger's drumsticks! I so desperately wanted one and I didn't get one, I was so fed up. But what a day!

I think it was one of the best days of my life.

Honestly, I could say that and people say, "Really?". Yes! It was a concert, but you don't know what it meant to me. Another great concert I went to was Roger Taylor at Manchester University.

I was there as well!

I was right at the very front at that!

So was I! [laughs]

I think we might have said hello. I can't remember, you know? I'd gone dressed in a long coat, like Roger's. I was stood there, at the front of the stage. Roger was singing and he looked at me and you know when you just get that eye contact? Then he just nodded his head at me and I went, "Ooooh!". I think I almost fainted!

We had our own newspaper and I used to sneak in a Queen connection. I would write a story like, there was this guy who opened a fishing tackle shop so I put in things like "If you feel like 'Lazing on a Sunday Afternoon'…" In every issue there was either a picture or a connection or something in a write up. Nobody knew about it, just select people.

We also set up a fanzine, which went all over the world, called 'Winged Messenger'. That was done by hand. We had a great big photocopier in the back room and just churned them out. That used to go to Affleck's Palace and in 'Record Collector'. It went off to 'Record Collector' magazine and we got reviewed. Again, it was just for the love of it, the passion. It's never really ebbed, it's always there. I go through Instagram in the morning and I'm like, "Morning Roger!" [laughs]

Denise Silcock was speaking to David Geldard.

Celluloid Heroes (With Just A Twist Of VT)
or, DUNG-DUNG-DUNG-DUNG-DUNG-DUNG-DUNG-DUNG...

Ken Shinn

It's late 1980, and I'm a big boy now. Well, one of the Lower Sixth, anyway. And dear me, I feel like an elite. The clod-hopping bullies of my earlier years in school have largely departed for the Forces or working in family businesses, and we now have – the elegant decadence of it! – a Sixth Form Common Room, where, between lessons, we loll like potentates on second-hand armchairs beneath posters of atomic bomb blasts and tanned, topless women with large breasts. And, of course, dazzlingly witty conversations and excoriations of all things, including popular culture.

One afternoon, I hear 'Jock' McKeegan holding court on a certain new record release, which has recently made an initial splash in the Top 40. I don't really listen to the chart show that much – I have access to a record player and my beloved soundtrack albums (BBC Space Themes, the Star Wars and The Empire Strikes Back double albums, a Geoff Love album or two of 'Sci-Fi Themes'… all of the good stuff) to form the required listening to my last-minute homework. He doesn't seem favourably impressed by the song in question, raising his voice to a squeaky, mocking falsetto to inform the assembly that 'we only have 14 hours to save the Earth'! As the discussion goes on, new mockery is added – 'Is he really just a man?', said in the manner of the Shangri-Las or The Damned at the respective openings of 'Leader Of The Pack' and 'New Rose' (a palpable misquote, as I soon discover), and, in particular, the low, urgent chant of 'DUNG-DUNG-DUNG-DUNG-DUNG-DUNG-DUNG-DUNG', which becomes a catchphrase of much mirth – even, in fairness, to me.

The record in question is, of course, 'Flash' by Queen.

I wonder if most of the mockery that my peers subject it to is down to it being – well – for a silly SF film. A lot of them love Queen – the group that still aren't as huge as they will be in a year or two more, but are already very well-known and loved by a lot of the said peers. Oh, how we chortled at the shock on the Headmaster's face when one bunch of jokers snuck 'Death On Two Legs' into one of their form assemblies, purely to get that reaction from 'but now you can kiss my arse goodbye...'. How we delighted in their heavy rock sound mixed with some of the most pretentious and impenetrable lyrics you could find. They seemed to be the perfect band for that most insecure yet arrogant demographic, sixteen-year-old boys. And now they were doing this daft, panto rubbish? Oh, how the mighty have fallen!

Nonetheless, as the Token SF-Loving Weirdo Of The Lower Sixth, it is of course my sacred duty to go and watch the 'Flash Gordon' film once it hits my local flea-pit, the Majestic in King's Lynn. When it turns up there in early December of 1980, I'm there. I'm not the oldest member of the audience, as there are a lot of families there. Many of them young families with young children, the kind who delight in loudly commenting on every bit of the unfolding action onscreen and laughing loudly at what are clearly meant to be dramatic points. It irks me at first, until I remind myself forcibly that I was just like that less than a decade ago. And guess what? It works! I love the film, in all of its camp-as-Christmas, comic-strip, goodies-versus-baddies, tinselly, swashbuckling, laser-blasting glory. And a large part of that is down to Queen's music.

Dung-dung-dung-dung-dung-dung-dung-dung…

Well, yes: but that's only a tiny part of the whole. And do you know what else? In the context of the story being told, it's absolutely perfect. It's a harbinger, a threatening, pulsing, approaching thunderhead of a riff, as unworldly and unsettling and thrilling as the crimson clouds of Ming's storms of Hot Hail billowing shockingly over a clear and cloudless sky. And, as I say, it's just the one small fraction of the whole shebang. A certain soundtrack album goes straight onto my Christmas list.

And, a few weeks later, I tear off the wrapping paper and behold that gorgeous, eye-searingly yellow-gold cover, with its starkly contrasting red planet/lightning bolt design. Knowing that the music may not be to everyone's tastes in my family, especially on a day of Christmas songs and Bond on the box, I ensure that I can make time to seclude myself in my bedroom for an hour or so and listen to the whole thing properly.

Odd thing about listening to it in such a way. The soundtrack album somehow provides me with a full audio-visual experience: the music in my ears, and the film playing out again on the screen of my imagination. And it's an enhanced and adrenalised version of the film that I'm watching.

How best to describe this? Maybe track by track.

One notable point about this album: like my beloved 'The Story Of Star Wars' LP, it contains not just music, but dialogue samples and sound effects. So, we open with an unearthly humming, interrupted by the weary, elegant tones of the Emperor Ming, and the oiled obsequiousness of Klytus. 'What plaything can you offer me today?' 'The planet... Earth!' And...DUNG-DUNG-DUNG-DUNG-DUNG-DUNG-DUNG-DUNG... 'Flash's Theme' – basically the single 'Flash', re-jigged slightly – crashes in: bombast, urgent keyboard runs, majestic guitar, and Freddie (and, lest we forget, Brian) hurling in some of the most breathless, overwrought vocal work imaginable. It is completely cheesy, and completely glorious: a marvellous, overbearing overture of a song.

'For God's sake – strap yourselves down!' Zarkov's urgent instructions, and the launch roar of a spaceship, aptly rocket us into 'In The Space Capsule (Love Theme)'. Opening with a wistful twang of guitar, we move rapidly into an ambient swirl of unearthly wonder, and under it all a pulsing drum beat, driving us onward like the fast current of some celestial rapids, on our whirlpool, kaleidoscope rush through the galaxy to Mongo. The sinister voices of Klytus and his Overseers welcome us to our destination – 'Bring it in safely. LAND it' – as 'Love' gives way to an ominous, bombastic crash of an ending.

'Prisoners! March below me to the presence of Emperor Ming.' The escort robot's nasal peremptoriness leads us to the very heart of Evil, in 'Ming's Theme (In The Court Of Ming The Merciless)'. There's an odd, unsettling, somehow subterranean quality to this piece – in fact, it reminded me of a contemporary ad campaign for a well-known bleach – which is somehow appropriate for this terrible tyrant, this infection of Existence. Sinister, insidious synthesiser prowls and leers, while the throb of imperious drums drive the piece to an abrupt, shocking climax. 'Death to Ming!' No chance. Not yet. Poor Prince Thun.

'Who are you?' Klytus brooks no delay, and, as our heroes give their names, Ming's mind is also on moving things forward quickly. With the sinister whine of what we'll call Ming's Ring Sting (heard whenever Ming puts his magic ring to use, you sordid souls), 'The Ring (Hypnotic Seduction Of Dale)' does what it says on the tin in less than a minute, deploying a creepily ethereal version of Ming's theme, with able help – much more overt than in the film – from Melody Anderson's purrs and occasional orgasmic gasps. And she looked such a nice girl!

'Forget it, Ming! Dale's with me!' Well, Flash isn't having any of that. Without preamble, we charge straight into the main segment of 'Football Fight'. Belligerent synths dash us along, cymbals crash and smash in time with the rucks and the punches, and triumphant guitar swaggers along as Ming's courtiers enjoy a rare moment of rebellion in support of this unlikely new champion. Ming's brutes appear more ominous in my mind's eye, their embarrassingly goofy teeth (which, I've just realised, are meant to look like gum shields – of course!) replaced with filed spikes. I've always liked my villains, even the stupid ones, to be suitably threatening. But Flash gives them a good run for their money, until a mis-thrown 'football' cracks him on the noggin and down he goes.

'It's just a bad dream...' But it isn't, Flash. 'In The Death Cell (Love Theme Reprise)' gives a new wistfulness to the piece, as we fear that we're witnessing the end of Flash, and an abrupt end to any love between Dale and himself. Reinforcing this, thudding, funereal drum beats punctuate the music as Flash is led to his death by poison gas.

The said death comes in surprisingly mellow, sinuous form, as the 'Execution Of Flash' is embodied by slithering, shimmering guitar notes, swirling and inevitable as the clouds of chemical death which they soundtrack, before the track ends on a sudden, blaring howl of despair and defeat.

Or is it? Of course it isn't. Ming's daughter Aura, and the Doctor who's one of her many lovers, have conspired to merely render Flash unconscious until he can be safely spirited away. But naturally, Aura is determined to big herself up as much as possible in his eyes, and thus 'I brought you back'... 'The Kiss (Aura Resurrects Flash)' is notable for some beautiful, wordless singing from Mercury, and Howard Blake's help with the music here provides a memorable piece of sensual bliss.

But, in any good pulp adventure, there's only so much time for the mushy stuff.

'You are playing with fire, Aura.' Despite the intensity of Barin's words, we enter into an oddly calm piece of atmospherics, more of an ambient aural picture of lush, quietly steaming vegetation, as we find ourselves visiting 'Arboria (Planet Of

The Tree Men)'. 'Lower them into the swamp!' And the darker side of this green paradise is revealed harshly with more throbbing, slushing percussion and synths, as we follow the marshy travails of Flash's 'Escape From The Swamp'. And that escape prepares us for things to go right through the melodramatic ceiling. A large chunk of the narrative is cheerfully skipped, and…

'I'm lost, Aura. Nothing can save me now!' Except, maybe – Flash! Ah-AHHHHHH! Yes, it's 'Flash To The Rescue'. Dung-dung-dung-dung-dung-dung-dung-dung! Throw in more sinister atmospherics as he lures Ming's flagship, the Ajax, into following him in a daring game of rocket-cycle chicken/chase-me, culminating with foreboding electronic throbbing as we pass through a massive, swirling crimson cloud bank, to hear the inspiring bellow of…

'Squadron Fourteen – DIIIIIIIIIIVE!!!' 'Vultan's Theme (Attack Of The Hawk Men)' is where my imaginary version reaches a real zenith. Rather than the impressive but undeniably creaky-looking flapping wings of the 'real' take, the music here is joyously fast, limber, acrobatic – the Hawk Men that it conjures up in my mind's eye flip through the skies, turning on the head of a pin in mid-air, soaring, plummeting, spinning on the breeze in their relentless onslaught. Imagination for the win.

'Stop all engines! Repel boarders!' And, after that airy fantasia, 'Battle Theme' brings things viscerally down to the crunch and thud of a pitched hand-to-hand struggle. Guitar stabs heroically, synthesised horns blare out halloos, drums rattle out a suitably pugnacious rhythm as Ming's garishly-clad troopers and stiff-winged Hawk

Men knock seven bells out of each other, as their hapless, lifeless bodies spin off towards unknown terrain far below... ray guns hiss venomously, Vultan guffaws as he smashes and gut-barges his way through the opposition, until finally Biro enthusiastically exclaims, 'Detonate the mine!' Flash is only too happy to oblige, and the track concludes with a literal bang, and the sound of the victors eagerly heading inside Ajax to take control, monitor transmissions from Mingo City, and...

A familiar, usually friendly, but unsettling tune blasts over the speakers. Here comes the bride... 'The Wedding March (based on Bridal Chorus)' sounds as joyous as it should, until doomy, minor chords underlie the melody, before resolving in a crescendo of somehow queasy joy once more. Ming and Dale are set to get hitched, and Flash can't let that happen!

'Until such time as you grow weary of her...' With the ring all set to be placed on Dale's fair finger, Flash's theme crashes in again – Ah-AHHHHHH! – but now, it carries, again, an almost desperate undertone – symbolic as such a gesture may be, if the 'Marriage Of Dale And Ming (And Flash Approaching)' – 'WHAT do you MEAN, Flash Gordon approaching?...' - is consummated, then it surely spells the end for all that is good...and desperate situations call for desperate remedies...

Sure enough, that DUNG-DUNG-DUNG-DUNG-DUNG-DUNG-DUNG-DUNG riff takes hold. Squares its jaw. Grits its teeth. Becomes, among the venomous pulsing of laser blasts, more and more strident, more and more insistent, before giving way to an enormous, thundering drumroll, as the 'Crash Dive On Mingo City' begins – and reaches its cataclysmic conclusion, with the nose spar of the Ajax buried squarely in Ming's vile back! As he slumps and fades from sight, his lethal escort robot appears once more…

'Hail, Flash Gordon, Saviour of the Universe…' 'YYYYYYYAY!!!' And, smash-cutting from Flash's triumphant freeze-frame leap (duly commemorated on the back of the album cover), we learn once more that he'll save every one of us, as 'Flash's Theme Reprise (Victory Celebrations)' plays us out, over the rejoicing and the reflections of the many amazing saviours of the Earth that we've come to know and cheer along the way. There's nothing like a happy ending, is there?

A chill wind blows. A hand reaches out. And the dreaded sound of Ming's Ring Sting shrieks forth once more, accompanied by the Emperor's echoing, disembodied, and thoroughly evil mirth! Oh my! It seems that the battle isn't over yet… A good thing, then, that 'The Hero' will be there to help us, come the day… and, as Mercury's victorious vocals assure us, 'Well, I tell you, my friend, this may seem like the end, but the continuation is yours for the making…' A marvellous instrumental outro ensues: from a stirring reprise of the 'Battle Theme', before segueing into a truly ominous rendition 'Ming's Theme', before 'Flash's Theme' sings us out, reassuring and heroic once more, culminating in an almighty, rolling clap of thunder.

I'm left exhilarated, overwhelmed, by the whole experience. What a rush! Even as I prepare to rejoin my family for the rest of a splendid Yuletide, I know that I'll be returning to this album again and again. Much as I loved the film, somehow, Queen's music, and some carefully-chosen dialogue, distils and refines it into something even more theatrical and melodramatic. I can even forgive the occasional jump in the narrative. Perhaps the best way to describe it is that I'm reminded irresistibly of Jeff Wayne's musical take on 'The War Of The Worlds' – another piece that uses powerful music to summon up the most marvellous of images, in the eye of the mind and, in particular, the imagination. 'Flash Gordon', the soundtrack album, is the ultimate huge-budget, spare-absolutely-no-expense, everything-and-the-kitchen-sink version of the tale: an epic, incredible achievement. In case you hadn't realised, I loved it then and I love it still, over 40 years on.

The past fizzles. Crackles. Distorts. Three years pass in the blink of an eye, and we find ourselves in October of 1983. The curtained sweep of the cinema screen shrinks down to the constrained spectacle of the cathode ray tube. I begin my second year of University, and a record is suddenly released, recorded in a frenzied two days of April that year. Brian May, it seems, has not had his fill of Space and science fiction, perhaps unsurprisingly given his keen interest in astronomy. And his son, Jimmy, has introduced him to the puppetry wonders and exploits of the crew of X-Bomber, or, as they're re-named for the dubbed UK version… 'Star Fleet'.

'Tell the people back at Earth Control – send Star Fleet legions to save our souls…' Purely for the joy of it, Brian assembles a supergroup including Eddie van Halen and Roger Taylor, and they jam on three tunes, releasing them as the Star Fleet Project. Only one track need concern us – the opener, a cover of the theme from the show, which does what any good interpretation by a band with members of Queen involved should do – it takes what was good about the original song, composed by Paul Bliss, breaks it down into its component parts, streamlines them, supercharges them, reassembles them – and then launches the whole shebang. And how! May and his chums come up with a deranged, almost fevered overhaul of the original, guitars screeching and wailing, vocals amped up into near-delirious harmonised yelling. It may just be a bit of fun, but dear me it far outdoes the original – and, again, all because of Queen's love of SF and Fantasy. While others groove to Haircut 100 or Kajagoogoo, I blast off with the Project.

Oh dear. Please excuse the static bars, there's a lot of drop-out on this tape. That's playing something too much for you. Just let me stop and eject that, then I'll get out my scissors and sticky tape, and splice this next reel of celluloid up for you. There will now be a short intermission, during which you may purchase small ice creams in large boxes from the foyer, and three years will pass in the blink of an eye…

All back in your seats? Good! Dim the house lights, and let's project… 1986. A new cinematic wunderkind has emerged from the Antipodes, and he's made his first Hollywood film. And Russell Mulcahy has produced quite the confection. A centuries-spanning fantasy battle of Good and Evil, with a mysterious but invaluable Prize awaiting the victor… 'Highlander' breaks new ground, in sheer visual style if nothing else, for SF/Fantasy cinema, and it's decided that, besides the orchestral talent of Michael Kamen, the already excellent score needs just that little extra kick – a quickening, one might say. And, of course, there's only one band that can fit the bill for those sorts of songs. Queen.

'Highlander' doesn't have an official soundtrack album as such (something which is true to this very day), but there is something close, Although a third of the tracks have nothing to do with the film, 'A Kind Of Magic' contains six cuts which all appear, to greater or lesser extent, at various points. And perhaps the best way to look at them is to consider them in the order that I think that they work best – largely, though not entirely, in the order that they appear in the film, not on the album itself. I'm kinda awkward that way.

'No one has ever known we are among you... until now.' Sean Connery's portentous tones end. The briefest pause. Then, the bold, challenging declaration: 'Here we are – born to be kings...' The opening credits rage across the screen to 'Princes Of The Universe', and, much as I love Queen's music, dare I admit to feeling a little underwhelmed by this song? It's fine, but it all feels a bit Queen-by-numbers. There's an oddly predictable feeling to it, and that's something that I don't expect or particularly want from them. Yes, it's bombastic, yes, it's overblown, but somehow it's all a tad soulless. Ah well. It's only the opening credits. Maybe things will pick up as the plot thickens...

'Just one year of love is better than a lifetime alone...' 'One Year Of Love', heard during a bar scene in the present day, is – despite its slow pace, perhaps because of it – oddly refreshing. A gentle, deliberately romantic piece, it's mellow, heartfelt, and tenderly optimistic. After the crash and flash of a lot of what's come before in the film, it plays its part to perfection in a brief oasis of peace for Connor and Brenda. Its very understatedness gives it a pleasingly idiosyncratic quality. That still, small voice of calm has a power of its own.

'Who waits forever, anyway?' Although it's also a love song at its heart, 'Who Wants To Live Forever' can't help but be a lot more powerfully affecting. Even apart from the resonances that it must surely have had with Freddie, facing up to the spectre of his own death just a few years later, it's a piece of strongly mixed feelings – the enormous, surging optimism of that 'and we can have forever', tempered by the resigned, almost pessimistic tone in which that last line is sung, followed by a quietly doomy series of descending chords, weary, despairing footsteps trudging through centuries. The crushing weight of Eternity has rarely been more keenly felt. It accompanies the most bitter-sweet and emotionally charged sequence of the whole film, and it's well-matched.

'I know his name…' And wham, we're slammed straight into my favourite tune of the whole soundtrack – on some days, my favourite Queen track of them all. Imagine my surprise when I read up a little on 'Gimme The Prize (Kurgan's Theme)' and discovered that Mulcahy, Mercury and Deacon all despised the tune. How can this be? The track was apparently 'too heavy metal' for Mulcahy, but that's part of what makes it so very wonderful for me. It's an enormous, overblown, menacing piece of camp, ideally suited to one of cinema's finest villains of all. This, for me, is up there with the 'Imperial March,' 'Ming's Theme', or 'Goldfinger' as the best theme tune of Evil ever. Throw in the crazed swirl of synthesised bagpipes in the bridge, and only one more thing can improve this further. And we get it. As with the 'Flash Gordon' soundtrack, this is the one cut of Queen's from Highlander that included dialogue samples. Better still, Clancy Brown dialogue samples. The presence of Clancy Brown automatically makes anything at least 20 times better. I can probably prove this to you, with diagrams and everything, if I ever need to. Or I can just play this track at you, at full volume and beyond. Cranked up to 11. Your argument is irrelevant.

'If you make it to the top, and you wanna stay alive...' By now, the songs have long left any pretence at gentle, wistful lyricism behind them – the film, both on screen and in my imagination, has built up a thunderhead of steam and it's gushing out like a geyser now. It's headlong from here until the crisis is over, and 'Don't Lose Your Head' – pounding in on an apocalyptic crash and rumble of drums to match Brenda's door disintegrating under the Kurgan's onslaught – is no disappointment in this regard. This is the perfect song for a breathless, adrenaline-driven rampage to the final confrontation, and fittingly enough that's exactly what it is in the film. It is a shame that we're denied Queen's camped-up scream through 'New York, New York' on the album version, but hey – we'll always have the celluloid. Oh, and Joan Armatrading's wordless, soaring vocal cameo is the icing on the melodramatic cake.

'This rage that lasts a thousand years will soon be done...' One big, final (well, apart from the sequels, the TV series, the cuddly toy...) confrontation later, Good has prevailed, and we learn that the Prize is apparently...the ability to have children and grow old. Which honestly doesn't sound like such a great trade for superhuman abilities and unageing immortality to me, but there you go. However, it does mean that we need one hell of an end credits track to go out on. And oh boy, do we thankfully get it! From its sly, finger-clicking opening onwards, 'A Kind Of Magic' delivers everything that you could want from a Queen number. Joyous laughter, soaring, gleeful vocals, guitar work that bubbles with pleasure – and, best of all, it doesn't just end. It fades gracefully, teasingly, out. As with 'Flash Gordon' before it, it says the continuation is very much ours for the making. Glorious, playful, optimistic, and I love it.

Oh! Where was I at the time? Well, I was in a platonic relationship with a marvellous young Goth – and, as well as Goth stuff, she loved Laurel and Hardy and 'Highlander'. One loose-end Saturday, I took a train trip to London (where she lived) with a quad poster for the film – Norwich had a wonderful shop where you could buy genuine film quads for a fiver a pop – with romantic notions of delivering it to her by hand. Alas, she was out, but her parents were in, and lovely people as well. She was apparently miffed to have missed me, but delighted by the gesture… I did meet her in person some time later, at her wedding. Wherever you may be now, Maxine, I hope that you're still married, and still happy. And that you still carry a torch for the Kurgan!

A little later that year, that Norwich shop provides me with another quad for my collection: for a film which attracts a lot of mockery, even hostility, from the purists. Even I regard it as a fascinating folly at first – something that I love in spite of itself. As the years pass, the film gains a bit of a cult reputation for itself, and I find myself loving it more for what it is. It's never going to be seen as a celluloid classic, but hey – neither is 'Flash Gordon', or 'Highlander', come to that. Like them, it's an unabashed panto adventure of Good against Evil – charismatic villains to hiss, eccentric mentors to love, and somewhat stolid but attractive principal boys and girls to aww for and cheer on. Gauche yet glorious, it is, of course, 'Biggles: Adventures in Time'.

And, once again, a part of Queen is there to add that little extra aural thrill and fillip. This time, John Deacon joins forces with Lenny Zakatek and Robert Ahwai, and they dub themselves The Immortals – perhaps a sly hat-tip to 'Highlander' there? Their song, the single sleeve informs us, is the theme from 'Biggles: Adventures in Time': 'No Turning Back'. Blimey! I think: that breakneck, melodramatic, synth-drenched glory from the opening? I buy it without a pause. And, when I get it home and first place it on the turntable, I'm oddly disappointed.

'Look into the Future, you can't leave it to the hands of fate...' Because this is not that deranged piece of kinetic brilliance, which I later learn is titled 'Do You Want To Be A Hero?'. No, 'No Turning Back' is, in fact, the end credits track – not what I was expecting. But, on re-listening, I find my opinion of this song rising fast towards approval. It's filled with a hazy, almost hallucinatory quality to its instrumentation – the lofty, drifting dream of Flight – studded with punchy, choppy hits that pull our attention back to the deadly mission at hand in 1917. It's never going to have the lapel-grabbing impact of the real theme, but it's also got that soaring, graceful spirit of adventure in spades, in its own quiet way.

Through my teens to my early twenties, my love for the fantastic endured, and grew. In large part due to the things that I watched – but, just as importantly, the things that I heard. Queen provided some of the finest soundtracks to such fantasias that I've ever encountered – and, marvellously, encouraged my imagination to provide even better visuals in my mind's eye. Perhaps, in some small way, it's not too much to say that Queen has inspired my writing in the years that have followed, and will do so in those that yet lie ahead. You don't have to squint too hard to accept that, I reckon.

And, unbidden, that grand old riff swells again, on the internal speakers of Memory: the call to Adventure, the rallying cry of Imagination.

Dung-dung-dung-dung-dung-dung-dung-dung!...

The Spare Ticket

Mick Hoole

"Let me welcome you ladies and gentlemen, I'd like to say hello." My name is Mick Hoole, I'm 60, and this is my Queen story. It began in 1974, but like a Tarantino movie this part of the story takes place in 1998.

Dr Brian May was on tour with his band at the Ardwick Apollo in Manchester, I happened to have a spare ticket as the person I was originally going with had to pull out last minute.

Having contacted the Official Queen fan club to see if anyone make use of the ticket, I was put in contact with 'Uncle Hefty', the manager of an up-and-coming tribute band who, it turns out, were one ticket short for a member of the band. This was the beginning of a wonderful friendship and the start of many a Queen-related adventure. I became part of the crew for this particular band – off on tour as chief dogsbody.

Now to 2001. We played bars and clubs to various sized audiences which culminated in a support slot at the Ocean club in Hackney, opening for Spikes All Stars or SAS band. This was led very successfully by Spike Edney, Queen's unofficial fifth member. The event was the tenth anniversary of Freddie Mercury's death, and likely to be highly emotional but fun.

Our day started very early as we had a sprinter van full of equipment and had to be in London for about 10 am – travelling down from Cheshire was going to be no mean feat.

On the day I had many different roles –helping load equipment, buying the bands drinks, checking the dressing rooms to make sure everything had been cleared out so the "stars of the show" could get ready in peace.

At the very last-minute Brian May and Roger Taylor announced they would join the SAS band to play a couple of songs, and obviously this changed the mood of the place. Once the huge crowd outside found out that there maybe some very "special guests" the atmosphere became electric.

The show was a massive triumph, Brian and Roger were on top form, playing six songs in total, and this is where it got really good for me. Tasked with going back to the dressing rooms for one last check for equipment, I turned a corner and almost crashed into Brian.

For years and years, I often wondered what would be my first words would be to a member of my favourite band, but never did I think it would an apology. As it happened Brian was enjoying a beer but not chatting to anybody else, so I saw this as my opportunity and as it turned out we had a great chat about dear Freddie. I managed to mention the four occasions I had seen Queen live, and the fact the first time was twenty-two years earlier, on 24 November 1979. We talked about the Pizza Oven lighting rig and how hot it was under the rows and rows of lights. I also managed to tell Brian how, as a 14-year-old, I had heard Queen for the very first time at school when a classmate came into school with a copy of 'Seven Seas of Rhye', which we played in the sixth form common room on an old Decca record player.

After shaking hands with Brian, I wished him well and future success and hovered back down the stairs to the rest of the gang.

Before I close this little section of my ongoing 47-year obsession, I'd like to mention 1976-7. I had just started work in 1976 and discovered beer and girls, and the music of Queen was always at the forefront. I wish I had seen Queen before 1979, but I did come close in 1978: coming second in a 'Tiswas' competition and winning a copy of 'Queen's First EP'!

How Queen Helped Me Survive Adolescence

Fotini Drakou

In late November 1991 I'm a few days shy of turning 11 years old. I'm at my grandparents' home with my family, we're chatting and having a good time as always. The TV is on and it shows a train busting through a brick wall, then the same train rushing along the lines, then a band playing on it, a man singing next to a woman with dark painted eyes. "Oh no, not Mercury!" my dad says. The news announces Freddie Mercury's death. "He was awesome, unique," my dad says, staring at the screen, still in disbelief. I regard the man still singing on the TV with awe. I feel sad for his death but there's also something else that grips me right then and there.

There's a memory gap between that moment and the moment that followed a couple of years later, when I got my first Queen album, 'Greatest Hits'. I play and replay the songs, learn all the lyrics by obsessive headphone-listening – there's nothing even approaching the idea of internet in Greece in 1993. My grandpa gets me 'A Night at the Opera' for my birthday – this one also comes with a booklet, I'm amazed. Soon I have the entire Queen discography on CD, along with some bootlegs, books and records I dig out from the flea market in Monastiraki.

The first year in junior high finds me a complete stranger among kids who were classmates through the six years of primary school. That, combined with the fact that my hair decides to become a perfect breeding ground for lice, make sure I remain an outcast for three whole years. In this hostile environment I try my best every day to keep to myself, maintain my distance and draw as less attention as possible. When I fail, kids taunt me, call me names, tell me I'm dirty and smelly. All the while I take constant showers and attack my hair with chemicals to remove the infestation. Nothing works.

Nothing except the happy-go-lucky attitude of 'You're My Best Friend', the wistfulness of 'Long Away', the angst of 'It's Late' and the absolute explosion of 'Sheer Heart Attack'. While my adolescent days are a season in hell and an exercise in despair, my nights are well-spent learning each piece of Queen music by heart, so much so that even all these years later I remember the specific moment of the first time I heard this or that riff, specific feelings that they triggered. I carry Queen with me as a piece of armour. I ask my English teacher to explain the meanings of weird words I find in their songs, like "innuendo" or "master-stroke" or what on earth "I leave it to you, leave it in the lap of the Gods" might mean. I observe the band's progression, from the enticingly dark progressive rock of 'Queen II' to the disco experimentations of 'Hot Space', the pop joy of 'The Works' and the unique return to form of 'Innuendo'. I watch their epic story unfold, all the while knowing how it ends, going back to its beginning, again and again.

First love hits me unexpectedly at 14 and of course it's unrequited and 'You Take My Breath Away' is the best soundtrack a dramatic teenager could possibly ask for. I play it on repeat and I plead, "So please don't go, don't leave me here all by myself", tears are shed, my heart is breaking, I'm sure no-one's ever loved this way before and no-one will ever again – including myself. It's so sad and yet so pleasing. Freddie gets it.

And I get him. I practically owe him my life, after all. I start voicing my support of gay rights and visibility. In addition to doing something good, this gives me a better footing for myself, grows my confidence. I speak out at school, to my relatives, I send letters to newspapers or magazines when I notice something homophobic or racist.

I catch obscure screenings of the Freddie Mercury Tribute Concert at random hours on Greek TV. I cry my brains out every time. I try to discover meanings and connections in Queen's songs, those little details that build the band's mythology.

In 1997 the internet breaks out and our house is among the first to get a connection. I type the URL of Queen's official website, letter by letter, and then it starts loading in a painstakingly slow pace as I wait in awe. It has a light brown background, I remember to this day. Still hooked on analogue, I fill up my drawers with print-outs of interviews and articles I discover around the – then very limited – web. I find message boards, I talk to other people who understand me, I find penpals – finally, I find my tribe.

One huge lice problem solved and several years later, I still listen to Queen, their sound intertwined with an entire era of my life. And I often wonder what kind of a person I would have turned out to be without their fundamental influence.

Jeff Scott Soto Interview

Singer & musician Jeff Scott Soto has shared the stage with Brian May and Roger Taylor at Official International Queen Fan Club extravaganzas and is a member of Queen sideman Spike Edney's the Spike All Stars.

Jeff - I have been an admirer of your vocals for a long time, ever since a friend lent me his Yngwie Malmsteen cassette back in my school days. As a Queen fan, I particularly love your Queen covers. How far back does your love of the band go?

Thank you for that, means a lot having now been nearly 40 years since it all began for me! I will start with the irony of how Queen fell onto my lap and how they became so important to me. When I first heard 'Bohemian Rhapsody', it was an instant connection with me in the beginning as it was for many who latched onto them from that point onward. I was probably eleven and it was an 'odd' song, the opera section was far too advanced for my ears and I could not stand Rock yet so the only part I could relate to were the ballad-y portions. I knew of many Queen hits from then until high school but it wasn't until I heard 'Live Killers' for the first time and realised how many songs I did not know WERE Queen. It was then I went down the rabbit hole and discovered this was MY band all along, the one that had it all, did it all, unabandoned, unreserved, no walls, no boundaries!

How much of an inspiration was Freddie Mercury on your vocal style and is there anything in particular that you think you learned from him?

This was the thing, once I discovered the many faces of Queen, I finally found a figure that would be injected into my DNA for life as an artist. Hearing Freddie sing everything from soul, rock, metal, folk, funk, blues, jazz, opera, etc., it became clear my role models could all be rolled up into one!

This has been a blessing and curse for me as an artist and bandmate… I had a bar I was chasing, I had a band that helped me understand there should not be bounds or blinders in music. This had me dissatisfied in about every band I was in, I wanted what they did musically but no one around me shared that vision. Most bands were one, maybe two dimensional, I wanted 10, 15, 30 dimensions to my craft because of Queen.

So as a blessing, it always kept me reaching for more, but as a curse, I had to hop around through so many bands to even come close. To this day, I still have not achieved this, but it's ok, I have not inhibited myself musically because of it and can stand proud on my personal accomplishments… thanks to Freddie, Brian, Roger and John!

Do you have a favourite Queen album - and if so, why that particular one?

It changes through the decades, it used to be hands down 'Queen II', this was an album leaps above 'Queen I', the choirs were immense and sophisticated, the progressive nature of the material was beyond that of any Rock band for its time.

It was a precursor to 'A Night at the Opera' and 'A Day at the Races' but also served as the album that forced them to take the chances they did even on 'Sheer Heart Attack'. If having to choose between them all, I think 'Queen II' has to be the one for me.

Did you ever get to see them live and if not is there a particular video concert you love?

In a conversation with Brian a few years ago, I told him it was one of my life's biggest regrets, not seeing them live with Freddie. His reply to me was Freddie would have loved my voice and talent... this to me was validation and possibly more important to take with me than any show I might have seen Freddie performing at in person! As far as live releases, I would have to say one of my faves is the one from Budapest, I thought Freddie's voice was in top form there... coming in second was the Montreal live video.

The live set you did at the Queen convention was outstanding and won you a lot of respect with hardcore Queen fans. Your love of the band comes over really well on that. What are your memories of that event and did you have fun picking the setlist?

Haha, many thanks, it was a dream for me creating the setlist, especially the medley... as a diehard fan, 'we' know how Queen became known for their medleys. Some found it unrewarding to not hear an entire song they would start and not finish, I came to enjoy the ideal of being able to play more songs within your 90 - 120 minute set, especially deep cuts that only diehards would know.

At this point, most tribute bands I had seen stuck to the Wembley setlist, yellow jacket included...

I knew playing at a Queen convention, I could get away with playing 'Man From Manhattan' or 'Polar Bear' if I wanted to! But my main objective was to go deep, even do songs Queen themselves were not known for doing live… and making them sound believable!

I had my trusty backing singers Peter Walkinshaw and Richard Mace, also diehard fans like myself, excited about the songs chosen, the band were like 'what song is this, or that?', it was quite funny. Also, a man who would become my tour manager and father-figure, Frank Tunney, was also connected with the 'royals' there, his wife Jennifer to this day runs brianmay.com and these folks are truly my extended English family!

As far as the convention, it goes hands down as one of the most fun (and frightening) experiences onstage… fun because I was living out my Queen fantasy of performing all of these gems, frightening because if you stuff it up, you'll be taken the piss on for life, haha! To finalise this statement, Roger once told me [about watching the DVD] I knew their songs better than they did… once again, an 'I can die now' moment!

As an American Queen fan, was it frustrating that they had somehow lost fans because of the 'I Want to Break Free' video?

Yes, I get it, especially more now when you realise just how homophobic the US was during that time. Even for me, to see them dress as women after defending them for years 'they are not gay, they are just English' explaining their inhibitions and humour was beyond what we tolerated here. We all 'knew' Freddie was gay and for me it never mattered, as much as it didn't matter the others weren't. But even trying to explain it was a spoof lifted from another source, no one had ever heard of here, 'Coronation Street', it fell on deaf ears and this video along with 'Radio Gaga', killed the US's passion for Queen... pity, they let them 'go' before so much more greatness was to come!

Do you have a favourite Queen solo record?

It would have to be Freddie's 'Great Pretender'... 'Mr Bad Guy' was just a little too 'gay disco' for me I am afraid but some of the retakes using his voice over a new bed of music, even as they did on 'Made In Heaven', were fantastic! But Brian's 'Back To The Light' was damn good!

You famously sang with Queen when they received their star on the Hollywood Walk of Fame. What was the story behind that? What was it like to play with your heroes and were you nervous?

Not so much nervous as I was excited... The story behind is a rather lengthy one that's almost impossible to abridge, haha. It more or less started in '99 when I read an article that Brian was about to release his second solo album, 'Another World', and he mentioned he would not be touring for it this time after realising how brutal it was to sing and play an entire show/tour. I thought to myself, I wonder if Brian had a front man, someone who could sing the obligatory Queen and other songs, he could sing some of his from his albums and find a happy medium behind it? So, I ventured out to get an address where I could write to him, send him some songs, etc., granted, I had met him once briefly and almost forgettable at the launch party for 'Innuendo' in LA.

As I searched high and low I found another recent article on how Queen were possibly reforming for a future tour with a new singer, not yet appointed. I got even more excited to REALLY get some stuff to them somehow. The only person/place I could find to send anything was Jacky Smith who runs the Official Fan Club.

I sent an email to her explaining the above, no reply… sent a follow up a week later in which she finally replied that what I said had no validity, but if I wanted to send her some songs, she would be happy to have a listen. I compiled and burned her a disc and within ten days got an overwhelming reply saying she LOVED my voice and she will absolutely hand deliver this to Brian at his home but if I would please send her a copy to listen keep… haha, 1999, no one really had the means to copy CDs yet!

She did as she promised and within two weeks I received a lovely hand written letter from Brian who thanked me sending the songs, knew of me from Yngwie, complimented me on what I had sent but dispelled any rumours about a reunion. I wrote back and he wrote again, my rock star hero penpal was born haha.

Fast forward to August, Jacky reached out to me about a Freddie event the fan club were throwing and Brian would be guesting with the house band, Spike's All Stars. She said she could get me to sing an a song or two with Brian if I would make my way to England for it… many, many details in between that, but the main one is, I did make it, met Brian and Spike for the first time, and the bond was formed.

From there, I was invited to do a few things with Spike and then the call came about the Walk Of Fame in '01, that they planned a jam where Brian and Roger would be coming out to play. Thanks to Jacky, the entire friendship and bond I have with them today is all due to her hearing the passion this band injected in me, I am so proud to call them friends but coming back to your original question, I was never nervous. My confidence was built and formed by all they influenced me with so it was always a natural feeling with them onstage. Of course, the dream, the bucket list, the one position I would have love to have is the one Adam is currently ruling but I can still walk away with the bond that we started over 22 years ago!

If you had the chance to play with them again, what would you choose to perform?

Ha, that's the million pound question… there is no real answer, every one of their songs is sheer magic to me (see what I did there?), if I had to choose one, it would have to be a LOOOOONG medley, maybe a 90 minute song with 90 one minute versions sewed together… hell, that would be an entire show then… so that's my answer, 90 songs, 1 min each, and I could name them all for you if I had to!

Jeff Scott Soto was speaking to David Geldard.

Queen Always Kept Me In A 'Drowse'

Sue Duris

Many of my Queen friends would tell you that 'Drowse' is my favorite Roger Taylor-penned song, even though 'Sheer Heart Attack' will always be my favorite Queen album.

I've been a Queen fan since 1974. That's thanks to 'Killer Queen'. When I heard that song I was hooked. I fell in love with Queen the first time I heard that song.

I was too young to go to concerts, even though Queen would be so close to me in Saginaw, Michigan, in 1976 for their 'A Night at the Opera' tour. The year I wanted to see Queen, in 1977, when they would be in the US for two tours, 'A Day at the Races' and 'News of the World', I was still too young to see them live.

I was never too young to buy albums and read about them – as much as I could get that is – in my favorite music magazines, 'Creem' and 'Circus'. I actually loved it pre-internet when phone calls, writing letters to pen pals, and going down to your local record store to find out about and buy records of your favorite artists and buy concert tickets was life.

I didn't get to see Queen until the Jazz Tour at Cobo Arena in November 1978, when I was able to see Roger in his "tigerskin trousers", Freddie,

Brian and John. I was fairly close up and while it was only my second concert of all time I was in awe. The lights, the sound, the band! From that moment on, I knew a Queen gig wouldn't be just a rock concert, it would be an experience, a totally fab experience, and it was!

The 'We Will Rock You' fast version will always be my favorite, even though '39, 'Killer Queen', of course, 'Now I'm Here', 'Keep Yourself Alive', 'It's Late', 'If You Can't Beat Them' and 'Spread Your Wings' are favorite hits of mine that they played.

I've been fortunate to see Queen a plethora of times since, including in three countries. I was so fortunate to be at Queen's last concert in the US with the original lineup on 15 September 1982. The concert was held at the LA Forum. I was bummed too because the US lost them after that show. The original lineup would never return.

While they would come back to the US in different iterations – with Paul Rodgers and with Adam Lambert – since then, I wouldn't see them back at the Forum until 2019. The fabulous Forum is a magical place so I definitely can relate to the band's love of the venue!

Some Queen fans look up to me because I saw Queen with Freddie, but I tell them that I was terribly grateful to be at the right place at the right time to see the band. Some people don't ever go to rock concerts and live through Queen's music – whether that's audio, video or a combination. I count myself as one of the lucky ones.

Some things stood out for me at that show – Billy Squier, Roger and his beautiful chrome kit, the Freddie vocals and the strut, Freddie and Roger volleying back and forth on 'Action This Day', Brian playing magic on that red special. And who could miss John's dancing?!

This was the second time I had heard 'We Will Rock You' – the fast version – live in the arena and it was fab. Something I'll never see again. That version of 'We Will Rock You' was made for one Freddie Mercury! All of this combined with a stellar light show, what could be better?!

If I would have known this would be the last show ever in the states with the original lineup I would have not let the band leave. I would have kidnapped them all!

I was such a big fan of Queen's 'Hot Space'. Many think it was a mistake. You have to go down paths in life to grow. I wish I would have seen more 'Hot Space' shows. I love that the band ventured into funk. And I don't buy for a minute they didn't want to. Knowing Roger's love of funk, he, like myself, was an Ohio Players fan, and to hear some of his music like 'Two Sharp Pencils' and 'Turn on the TV', this band was born to venture into funk.

Forget about this concert not being as popular as the others, it was great music and any true fan would have loved this tour! It was also fab to hear some great songs from the catalog like 'Dragon Attack', 'Save Me', 'Action This Day', 'Now I'm Here', 'Tie Your Mother Down', and a regular favorite, 'Jailhouse Rock', which Billy Squier came back on stage for.

Even though not a sell out, the show was high energy, the band was really hot and quite energetic on stage and everyone was upbeat for the show, and that excitement showed throughout the arena. I remember the Forum really shaking!

It's a night I won't forget not just for the being part of history part, but to be part of a great concert experience with four blokes known as Queen!

I never met the band when they were touring, but I would meet the surviving members of Queen later in life.

A friend of mine recently posted about taking a time machine back to the early days and reliving every Queen moment. I'm definitely in on that. I was also chatting with another friend and we were talking about Queen lasting throughout time. Queen was able to navigate a changing musical landscape – punk, disco, new wave – and come out victorious. They had a plan, they stuck to it, and wouldn't let anyone put them in a box.

I remember when we lost Freddie, it was sad for me, it was sad to see others in pain, it was sad to see the band struggle. But we have to move on. And the band did. And I'm so grateful that Brian and Roger are still making music. And I'm happy that John is enjoying his life.

While I would lose touch with Queen, thanks to life, I would return to my love of this band. I moved to the UK not long ago and have done some Queen pilgrimages in the UK, Munich and Japan. It was inspiring to see places they performed, recorded, and lived.

Ultimately, 'Teo Torriatte' is my favorite Queen song. I got to see it performed by Brian and Queen + Adam Lambert in Tokyo in 2020. I can definitely see why the land of the rising sun fell head over heels in love with Queen. We all did.

As Freddie once said, they were a form of escapism for people to be entertained. I listen to my huge Queen – and other band member's projects – collection to reminisce, when a certain feeling hits me, and to enjoy really great music that will never die.

Long live Queen!

Gettin' Smile: Track by Track with Tim Staffell

Tim Staffell

The genetic composition of Smile was two parts 1984 (Hampton School Band) and one part The Reaction (a notable co-existent Truro based band), and the resulting trio contained characteristics of both bands in a hybrid concoction of heavy harmonic rock. It was a short-lived affair, but established an embryonic style of music which was later to evolve and grow into the world-class classic material developed by Queen under the stewardship of the charismatic Freddie Bulsara.

The recorded canon of the band is small, but notably eclectic; and displays some of the dynamics (and the sensitivities) to be found in the later works.

Although the material has ended up as an album, this is only due to expediency and the interest generated by the later successes; the range of songs is fairly broad, and I'm inclined to think that, accidentally, there's a reasonable balance of emphases; certainly fans appear to think so.

Each song has its own origin and derivation – as far as it's possible I'll try and elucidate those origins; (it should be understood that some of this is filtered through a half-century of questionable human memory – I'll bow to any contrarian factual assertion with good grace).

The track order of the original vinyl 'Gettin' Smile'

is as follows, and I'll deal with each tune in this order:

'Doin' Alright'

Clearly the most well-known of the tunes, recorded and existing in numerous forms to the present day; it represented Brian and my second foray into writing. At the tail-end of the sixties, it was becoming much more important for musicians to enhance their USP with original material – 'Smile' was our test-lab for the kind of material we liked to play. Although there aren't huge similarities between my subsequent output and Queens', it seems to me that there has been a common love of structure in our respective writing. 'Doin' Alright' has two distinct complementary motifs with a dynamic bridge. The verse is in a style I call a 'pedalled arpeggio' – with a drone note and rising triads, the chorus is a pushed heavy riff that carries the resolution of the tentative uncertainty of the lyric. I attempted to rethink it as a gentle country tune on my 2004 album 'aMIGO' but I don't know how well it works. I leave the listener to judge.

In 2018, We revisited the tune for the movie 'Bo Rhap'. The remit on the re-recording was to try to revisit the more visceral nature of the original 'Smile' recording, but in a modern context. I think we succeeded. Lyrically it's a general comment on the transition from personal angst to relief and positivity. People have said to me that they responded to the lyric as a reflection of their personal circumstances. I'm flattered by this. Mostly, one could say that Brian was responsible for the music, and I the lyrics (in general as a writing partnership, because Brian is a far better musician than myself)

'Blag'

I seem to recall that 'Blag' was based on an idea by Roger. Keeping in mind that these tracks were recorded without a clear idea of an album configuration, the premise was very definitely to portray that aspect of the band that had vitality and punch, and upped the energy level from some of the other material. After all, our mission statement was that we were a heavy rock trio with powerful intelligent harmonies. So 'Blag' was intended as a closer exposition of that style. Listening back to my vocal gymnastics, especially on this tune – I'm amused that it was so apparently fatally undisciplined in places. Lyrically I think less attention was paid to any kind of narrative – it's more a case of the voices as instrumental flavours than anything literate.

'April Lady'

Credited to a Stanley Lucas, but claimed by Carl Barnwell of (Matthew's) Southern Comfort and recorded in 1971 by them, though not with the novel time-signature. As I recall, Fritz [Fryer] introduced us to this tune; I'm not sure how we really felt about recording a cover in principle, but the mildly esoteric combination of 5/4 and 4/4 tempi was sufficient to persuade us that it would be good for our musical credibility in the marketplace. As it happens the chorus showcases the harmonies pretty effectively, and I think it integrates pretty well...

'Polar Bear'

At the time I was never really sure what to make of the lyrics, I think I found that they eluded me somewhat because they were so personal to Brian

– at the time, he was a big fan of penguins, (and I'm sure wildlife in general). I seem to recall wondering if it was at all allegorical, but that wasn't common in those days – except occasionally in the works of Bob Dylan – and we never discussed it, but again it illustrates attention to structure. The harmonies are amongst the most sophisticated that we had attempted at that time.

'Earth'

Harking back to the notion that original writing was becoming an indispensable weapon in the rock musician's arsenal, 'Earth' was the first of my own solo attempts that I felt confident enough to play to Brian and Roger. Structurally it's not so impressive as some of the other material – being as it is a conventional ii-V-I progression sequence – however the treatment and the harmonies give it a legitimacy over and above its simplicity. In those days I was pretty much a hardcore sci-fi buff (still am, really) and 'Green Hills of Earth' is a song mentioned in a number of the writer Robert A. Heinlein's novels. My song is only superficially similar to the Heinlein lyric, but the premise of an earthman marooned somewhere out among the stars after the demise of the homeworld was a strong image for me…I explored the idea further with 'Nova Solis' the title track of the album I recorded with the band 'Morgan'

'Step On Me'

Lastly – and this is my personal favourite from the album – 'Step On Me' harks from '1984' days… and I can't help but feel that because it had a longer history than the rest of the material, the arrangement and treatment just sounds more mature. For the time, in my view it was a classic top-notch pop tune, and had it been recorded by the right producer and marketed with enough passion it could have charted very highly, possibly both here and across the Atlantic. And then the story would have been perhaps quite different. But there you go – we were not the only band to fail to connect with the right PR; que, (as they say), sera, sera. Lyrically of course it's a conventional 'relationship tune' – boy (or girl) meets boy (or girl) – relationship turns sour, protagonist is dealt misery by the shedload… but it's a good song, and I'm sure is enjoyed by many people because of the appropriateness of the lyric to their own circumstances….

In spite of Smile ending with the proverbial whimper, the album is a reasonable archive of the development of the Queen musical 'vocabulary' – in my more self-important moments, I like to think that it represents a blueprint for a starship that I (we) handed to Freddie and more or less said, "Here you are, build this!" … there's a bit of truth in that, but really, that's just me bigging my part up; it represents a sketch in a notebook, that Queen honed into a genre all of its own; I took a different path… clearly not so marketable or iconic. I've said it several times, that it's just as well I moved on, because the eventual development of the style required skills and disciplines that I've always doubted I could possess; I've remained pottering about in the musical suburbs where Queen built a fantastic Cathedral right in the centre of town!

Front Page News: Discovering (And Rediscovering) Queen

Georg Purvis

"Who's that strange-looking man with the star-shaped sunglasses?" I asked my mom. My parents had divorced in January 1991, and all that meant to eight-year-old me and my younger sister was two Christmases. My mom, sister, and I moved in with my grandparents, but by November the novelty of living there had worn off; feeling sad and lonely, I went to my mom's bedroom to whine, but she was working at her drafting table, so I sat on her bed and watched VH-1 which happened to be reporting on the death of Freddie Mercury. When they showed a clip from the 'We Will Rock You' music video, the dots all connected: so this was the chant my friends and I shouted on the playground!

To her credit, my mom did her best to answer my question and educate me on Queen, but, given that we lived in the suburbs of Philadelphia, they weren't exactly on the average American's radar by this point. She rifled through a stack of cassettes, plucked out one with four bright-colored squares on it, and suggested I listen to it. I took it to my room, set it down, and forgot about music for the next two years.

By the time of my 10th birthday, we had moved to a new house my mom worked hard to buy all on her own. She was house-poor but we were happy; I expected nothing for my birthday, and was delighted to find a cassette boombox and three tapes: 'Happy Anniversary, Charlie Brown!', Eric Clapton's 'Unplugged', and Queen's 'News of the World'.

I loved all three cassettes equally at first, but gravitated towards the one with the creepy robot mauling four glam/art rockers. While the inner sleeve – the robot is now smashing through a cavernous venue as thousands of concertgoers flee, screaming – likely contributed to a lot of nightmares, the music across the 44 minutes of tape (I had the Hollywood Records version, with the Rick Rubin "ruined" remix of 'We Will Rock You' as a bonus track – I actually have a fondness for that song!) changed my life.

I had been gravitating towards music by this point – for some reason, 'Tears In Heaven' was all around me at that time, hence one of my gifts – but was still a child: Santa brought me New Kids on the Block's 'Hangin' Tough' and a My First Sony Cassette Player in Christmas 1988, but that clearly wasn't "serious" music. By the time I reached my double-digits, I was ready to put childish playthings behind me, become an adult, and take music seriously.

I have no idea where I got such a pretentious attitude towards music, but I latched onto Queen like they were a lifesaver, and I had to know everything about this band. Over the next few years I became an obsessive collector, grabbing every recording, book, and magazine I could; by the time I had saved up enough for a CD player, I replaced my worn copy of 'News of the World' with a fresh compact disc. I even bought my first bootleg CD – 'The Ultimate Back Catalogue Vol. 1' – at a poster shop on the Ocean City boardwalk. My dad fronted me some dough so that I could hear poorly-transferred recordings of 'Smile', 'Larry Lurex', and a handful of B-sides and extended versions.

Queen also introduced me to other musicians and bands: reading about their influences or collaborators in biographies, I would return from my local record shop, Trac Records, with a stack of new tapes and CDs. Before long, I was a Beatles obsessive, and after securing a copy of the first 'Anthology' on the day of release, I moseyed over to the "Q" section as a laugh to see if a new Queen album had been released. Keep in mind that I didn't have Internet at this point, nor was I up on the latest Queen news, as I figured that because Freddie was dead, there simply wasn't any. Imagine my surprise when I saw the cover of 'Made In Heaven' and a sticker that screamed "Eleven new tracks featuring Freddie Mercury's final recordings!" I didn't care about the Beatles anymore for that moment; I put back the 'Anthology' and instead purchased 'Made In Heaven' (hey, money was tight for a 12-year-old), then waited for my ride.

I couldn't even wait until I got home before I tore through the plastic and read the lyrics and liner notes. I consumed every title, every verse, every line, every credit, and I hadn't yet listened to a single note. "What does a song like 'Mother Love' sound like?", I wondered. "What an un-Queen-like title!" (Little did I know…)

Listening to 'Made In Heaven' for the first time was like listening to 'News of the World' for the first time: these were foreign songs to me, songs I was hearing for the first time, songs I had no background knowledge on. Okay, that's not necessarily true: I knew half of the album was made up of rejiggered solo tracks, but, by this point, I hadn't heard any of them, as 'Mr. Bad Guy', 'Shove It', and the 'Scandal' single were out of print; I was familiar with only 'Back to the Light', so I did have two versions of 'Too Much Love Will Kill You' to compare (and Brian May's is better).

But as the atmospheric keyboard and chirping birds of 'It's A Beautiful Day' washed over my boombox speakers, none of that mattered: I was hearing a new Queen album for the very first time, something I didn't think ever would happen. It was an emotional experience: every song was perfection, expertly performed, sung, and written, but I didn't understand some of the nuances of the songs, nor the 23-minute hidden track at the end and why they had wasted so much space on a bunch of weird sounds and chattering. I'd already heard 'Revolution 9', and didn't need to hear Queen's take on it.

Over time, I came to learn all that there is to know about Queen and their albums. For instance, that sound collage that 12-year-old me didn't understand was a moment of catharsis for the band at the end of the recording sessions, and is supposed to signify Freddie's ascent to heaven – or so I've been told! The magic has worn off by the ravages of time and curiosity; I've researched them to death, while other earworms have wriggled into my brain and other musicians have wrested me away.

But sometimes, if I'm in the right mood and the right song comes on, all that knowledge and familiarity dissolves and I'm taken back to those halcyon days of hearing that song for the first time with fresh ears. Sometimes I hear something I hadn't heard before; sometimes I'm hearing a song I didn't particularly care for before but can now appreciate in a new light; sometimes I'm just hearing it again after years of neglect. Now that's a kind of magic.

I Never Saw Queen Live

Gary Rothwell

I never saw Queen live. There, I've said it.

For many people this might be a casual comment, merely one of hundreds of bands they never saw... but I've been to nearly a thousand gigs.

I can't make the excuse that I was too young, which I can lob out as to why I never saw The Beatles, Led Zeppelin, or Sweet with Brian Connolly.

Nor can I claim they never played near enough when I know for sure that's not case on many occasions.

If I look at my list of "most records by" (and we all have one of them, right?), Queen sit proudly at number #9 (albums) and #6 (singles), so I can't make out that I'm only a casual fan, and so what if I didn't see them? To put it in context, you have to go to #30 before you find another band I could have seen live, but didn't.

I love them, and yet I never saw Queen live...

For someone who grew up in the '70s, there are bands that have effectively been there your whole life, same as your parents, your friends and 'Doctor Who'.

To grow up with a band such as Queen releasing great – and very different – singles every three or four months didn't seem anything out of the ordinary in the 1970s, I just accepted it as the norm.

Each month I'd take my pocket money and spend it on whatever the most recent single I liked was.

I'm not going to pretend it was always Queen, it wasn't. But often it was. I bought 'Killer Queen', 'Bohemian Rhapsody', 'Don't Stop Me Now', 'We Are the Champions' and a couple of others as they came out, and loved and played them to death.

I remember seeing 'Killer Queen' on 'Top Of The Pops', and sat transfixed watching the (not actually the first) first real promo video of 'Bohemian Rhapsody', bellowing out the operatic bit with random words which made absolutely no sense!

I'm a life-long glam fan, and we can argue forever as to whether Queen were glam or not, but for me, everything around that time somehow tumbles into the glam rock/pop umbrella. Whilst there were others who were more glam, and those who were glam for longer, there was surely no one more glamorous than Queen. Freddie played the part, looked the part and lived the part. The band wrote some of the finest rock and pop singles EVER. That is really an undisputed fact that will live on long after we're all dead and gone.

Apart from the classic singles, they also released fabulous, diverse and unforgettable albums, with a run of albums in the '70s equal to anyone else of the era. That's not to denigrate the '80s and '90s albums, which I also love… just not as much, but hey, we got to have a favourite era!

Of course I hated 'Hot Space', but I saw that as more an aberration than anything, and thought 'The Works' an excellent return to form. I keep thinking I must be wrong and every year or so I give it a spin. But I remain convinced I am right!

So why didn't I see Queen live?

By '86 I was living in Rusholme as a student in Manchester... just a stone's throw away from Maine Road, when they announced a gig for 16 July. I don't remember exactly when they went on sale, but I am thinking it was likely during the easter break when I was back home.

I was then – and am now – the one who checks what gigs are coming up, poised outside the venue, by the phone, on the internet, using an app (select appropriate method depending on your age). I left nothing to chance, I was always there, ready. I knew that if I didn't get tickets, I would have done all I could.

My mum slept outside the ABC Cinema in Huddersfield to see the Beatles back in '63, so she knew my pain.

I don't recall why I didn't see Queen on the 'Works' tour, but now was the opportunity, and I was set to head to Maine Road to queue up, as was my want, and yet somehow I was swayed by a good friend. "Don't worry," he said, "I'm staying back in Manchester, I'll go down and buy us tickets". That's what friends are for, of course! I was delighted, we'd been to plenty of gigs, and I'd queued up for tickets for him before, I was in good hands, nothing would go wrong.

I called him up in the afternoon to check where we were standing or sitting... he'd slept in... not got there in time. It was sold out.

Time has dulled my memory somewhat as to exactly how I reacted, but I was unhappy, very unhappy. I convinced myself later that all was OK, after all they'd be back round for another tour in a couple of years, I can see them then.

I think had I really thought about it, I could have just gone on the night and got a tout ticket… but I was just so gutted, I didn't

Since then I have, of course, purchased all their albums (numerous times), and I listen to then all on a regular basis (except 'Hot Space'… sorry), but if I had to pick a favourite it would be 'Sheer Heart Attack'. Love that album. It's got 'Killer Queen' (which I'd have go with as my favourite Queen single), 'Brighton Rock', 'Stone Cold Crazy', 'Now I'm Here', and the others you all know. For me it has the perfect balance of all the things they were great it. Great riffs, great melodies, the studio perfection, brilliant harmonies, and sounds effortless. And a super-cool album cover!

The moral of the story? If you really want a ticket, trust no one! If you get a chance to go and see someone you want to see, then go!

I never saw Queen live. And forty years later, it still stings.

Doin' Alright: The Doug Bogie Interview

Musician and sound engineer Doug Bogie was the third and last bass player (after Mike Grose and Barry Mitchell) before John Deacon joined Queen.

Long before you met Freddie, Brian and Roger, how did you get into music?

My first exposure to music was when I was aged 6 when I got a piano accordion and took lessons. How Scottish is that? [laughs] I can remember to this day playing 'Paper Roses which was a pop song of the era. Then I went to school and it was classical music, I went to one of those Grammar Schools that had been there for hundreds of years. It was a nice place but it was that way inclined, so it was the clarinet for me and I was terrible. My brother, who was six years older than I was, he was in a teen band, trying to look like Buddy Holly with the black rimmed glasses with the glass taken out so you could see. So, I used to mess around with his kit when he wasn't around, which I shouldn't have done but I was very keen on making a noise!

Like everyone else, I was completely enthralled with The Beatles. I didn't really know anything about the more rock n' roll stuff, The Rolling Stones didn't really mean anything to me except hit records and they were great. So, it was all very much The Beatles, for me.

Then my Dad bought an open reel tape recorder. I used to play with it. I would record things,

I discovered that by mixing tracks, you could make phasing noises and kind of got me into the technology of music really.

Then as I progressed through Grammar School it was Cream, John Mayall, Led Zeppelin and Yes. One of the other guys at school was into old blues, he turned up one day with an album, with this black guy on the cover called Big Bill Broonzy. Before you know it, we're all being very bluesy! It was great, I loved it.

I had the usual amateur band, sort of bluesy, we did cover versions of Rory Gallagher's 'Taste', a couple of John Mayall's tunes, we tried a few of our own but mostly people didn't care about the stuff that you wrote, they wanted stuff they could recognise. That was called Shadowfax, so I was an early adopter of the whole 'Lord Of The Rings' thing. That would be in the mid to late sixties, I suppose. The last Shadowfax gig was in 1969 at Esher Town Hall. We used to hire a more well-known band, so we could be the support and it worked out.

How did you become aware of Queen?

That's very simple. One of the things I liked to do, I quite enjoyed going to auditions. In the back pages of the Melody Maker, the weekly music paper, along with the adverts for Grandad shirts and bell-bottomed trousers, there was a page for auditions. So, I would look at some of them and think, "That sounds interesting" and then ring up. So, one of them was for these guys. It just said, "Bass player needed. Please ring this number". I phoned it up and I got given an address for the audition. The audition was at Brian's University lecture theatre. The building was right behind the Royal Albert Hall. At that time, I was living in Weybridge, with my Mum in a flat because my Dad had passed away and things weren't very good but we were surviving, you know? So I stuck my bass guitar in a rucksack and I jumped on the Green Line bus because I knew that bus went all the way from Weybridge, into London and actually went past the Albert Hall. In the end, I found my way into this lecture theatre with these hairy guys. What made it pleasant and a nice experience was they had a roadie called John Harris, who was a real gentleman. He was always the guy who hustled up the van, he was the guy who borrowed a bit of gear, he was just a nice bloke. He was lovely.

I can't remember the titles exactly but we started off doing some bluesy, rocky, riffy playarounds to warm up. I heard a couple of riffs, I think, if I remember rightly, it was 'Son And Daughter' and 'Stone Cold Crazy'. Then, I suppose, about an hour later, the door opens… and down the lecture theatre steps comes Freddie. He had Mary on his arm.

It's funny what you do remember, he was wearing what could only be described as a rabbit skinned jacket. It was fucking terrible! [laughs] But, it was great. It was 1970, the hippy stuff was still around and glam hadn't happened as such. People wore all sorts of weird stuff. It was very definitely an art student look. I have to say, he was not particularly friendly, but not particularly unfriendly either but very matter of fact. Then we just got into a couple of tunes.

Basically, a little while later, that was it, I was in! Then it was "When can you make the next rehearsals?". We did the rehearsals. I did do the hanging out a little bit. I went street walking with Roger. We walked around the centre of London.

There was a nice guy called Paul Conroy who worked at the agency part of Charisma Records. We went to see him a couple of times because he helped organise the gigs we were going to do. He was being a friendly, helpful guy. They were sort-of doing their networking thing. I went up to see Roger and Freddie's shop. You have to bear in mind I was only 17. This was amazing to me. This is what I had been daydreaming about getting into, it was great. Then we just prepped up for the two gigs.

How would you describe the guys individually, from what you remember?

Well, having been in amateur bands with other guitar players, I recognised what Brian was immediately. He was a slightly dark, moody, introverted guy like most people who are starting up playing instruments are because he's probably spent God knows how many thousands of hours hunched up over his guitar, learning his stuff, you know? Nothing I am saying here is an insult, it's just an observation of someone's personality type. He was very introspective.

Whereas Roger, again, like so many drummers, if anyone was going to be a 'Rock Star', to use the dreaded term, it was going to be him. Because he's got that cheeky-chappy, pretty-boy, great voice and what he does is very physical, he was a very outgoing person. He was great. I really took to Roger.

Freddie was not what he later became. He couldn't really sing any better than anyone else in a million and one other amateur bands. Again, this isn't an insult, this was the early days. He got better bloody quickly.

Can you remember much about the gigs you played with Queen?

Yes, the first one was at Hornsey Town Hall. Hornsey is in North London and the Town Hall is a great big Victorian building with a huge cavernous, echo-y hall. We were supporting The Pretty Things and The Pink Fairies who were fairly big in those days. As was tradition at the time, nobody really goes to see the support band, particularly if you've got a three-band gig on. So, the bar is always fairly full, even quite early on. You're on about 7:30 or something and most people haven't even thought about getting out of bed by then. In those days the lighting for these things was very basic, sometimes no more than a few theatrical lamps used for the general meeting of the local council. A guy would come in with his pals, with half a dozen slide projectors and they would project slides through wheels of oil. So, even the lighting when it was full on, it was quite low key. When you're the support, well, you get fuck all. The P.A. is turned up to number two instead of number twelve, you know?

It was very dark, there was probably only a dozen or so people there, just mooching about. So, really, my experience was, it wasn't really much more than a rehearsal, because we're up there on the stage, Freddie is basically standing with his back to the empty room. He was really singing to Roger and Brian; I'm just there doing my stuff and that was kind of... about it. We did a short set and then we were out of there and back in the van, which was borrowed. John Harris had sorted the van. We're sitting at the back of the van on the floor and that was done.

I wouldn't say it was crap, it was just what you would expect from a support band of that era.

Did you get any feedback from it?

No, not at all. I don't think they would have been very pleased about being ignored, playing in the dark and not having an audience. In all fairness, I can understand that. I've done amateur gigs before now, in my local college in Kingston upon Thames, where you were lucky if you had twenty people. Bear in mind, they'd also had a year of trying to get going and it hadn't really been happening. They'd lost their bass player of several months which obviously didn't help. So, they probably were not in a great place mentally.

So how did the next gig go?

Well, then we had what I'm going to call 'the proper gig' at Kingston Polytechnic, my home ground. That was supporting Yes. Now, I'm a massive Yes fan! I love the first album in its jazzy, weird way but the second album… I won't call it religious but it was pretty bloody close! It was great.

That was an interesting day for all sorts of reasons. I didn't meet up with them beforehand, I just went there on my own because that was only three miles from where I stayed, a place called Hampton Court, just down the River Thames.

So, 'The Yes Album' is big and they're just back from a tour of America and they've brought back a P.A. system. Do you know what I mean when I say cinema bins?

Yes!

They had bought back this bin system from Iron Butterfly. This was the first time I'd seen a big 'eff off P.A. It's not a huge hall, so four big bins with some great big horns on top were really amazing.

And they had a mixer at the other end of the room, WOW!

They were made by a company called Altec Lansing. It had big knobs and meters on, stuff you hadn't seen before, except in a picture. I was knocked out because, as you know, I love the technology. It was all looking good but then we get told, "No, you're not bringing on your shitty, crappy amps". So, we were obliged to plug into Yes's backline. Now, I was happy with that because I had a shitty old amp anyway. I, me, 'Mr. Nobody', I'm about to plug my tatty old, not even a real Fender Telecaster Precision (it was a European lookalike), I'm about to plug it into Chris Squire's Fender Dual Showman amp. Two Dual Showman amps, each one with a Dual 15" Speaker Cabinet, that was the total Rolls Royce of kit in those days. It was worth several years of income to me. So, I was as happy as Larry. Brian was a bit more 'Humpty Tumpty' because, of course, a Fender Dual Showman sounds nothing like a Vox AC30.

So, it was an ordinary college, it was a theatre, stage and a few wee rooms behind. We were in one of those rooms, using it as a dressing room. Then it turns out we were in the wrong one, we had to move because when the guys from Yes turn up, that's the one they were going to have. Then, I'm not sure who it was, someone said it was Chris Squire, had a wee go at Brian for playing the piano.

Anyway, we didn't get much of the audio or the lighting but it was much, much better. It felt like a proper gig to me. Now, I probably had twenty or thirty pals in the audience which helped me as well. So, I was just doing what I normally do. I was a 17-year-old, I was leaping about and having fun. I always thought bass players should have fun.

I thought everybody on stage should have fun. What I wasn't aware of, is that some people don't share that point of view so much.

I thought it was great. I thought it was a brilliant night. Excellent. Then we finished. I'm happy. Again, we're getting back in the van with the kit and Freddie just goes off on a total rant. He just goes off, "That was rubbish! That was shit! I have never heard anything so appalling!".

I've got to tell you by the way, that Freddie was better that night. He actually faced the audience. Brian was still very introverted. When he played, he was very 'head down' and not very outgoing at all, but it was much, much better.

Freddie was going on about how awful it was, terrible, he couldn't possibly deal with it anymore and this band is finished! So basically, I was never fired from Queen, Queen just stopped. Now, were they lying to make me feel better? I don't know. So, I can't really tell you the real story about that. It has been said to me by people who are supposed to be in the know, that Freddie thought I was trying to upstage him. Because, at that time, he wasn't the outrageous performer he became two or three years later. So basically, that was the end of my collaboration with Queen, because as far as I was concerned, they were finished. But there are some other links throughout my life.

It's sad that it ended like that but you still worked in the music industry after that, didn't you?

I thought it was a shame, but bands come and go all the time, so I just started another one, a local band. We gigged and had fun. I also managed to get a job then, within the year I suppose it would be, I'd be 18, at De Lane Lea Studios. I really did spend a year writing letters, knocking on doors, making phone calls and trying to get into a recording studio was difficult. But I managed to get a job as a tape operator which means glorified tea boy and runnerarounder but that's how it starts. I was very lucky because it was a great studio. If I tell you that my first major project was E.L.O. on my third day…

Bloody hell!

…it was pretty hot, you know what I mean? I had a good time. So, I was working with Roy Wood and Wizzard and his other band, Eddie and the Falcons. I'm actually on 'I Wish it Could Be Christmas Everyday' because we all got into the studio and were singing along. Just crazy stuff like that. It was a great place to work plus because they had the big, big studio we were doing movie soundtracks too. So some rock n' roller would be in there one day and some movie star the next, it was great!

One day I was in the tape library, mooching about like you do and I come upon demos by Queen. Bear in mind this was 1971,72. Which at that point, of course, no one had heard because they only got out years later. I thought, "That's interesting, so they did do some more!". It turns out, you probably know the story, they were allowed to record in there when they were practising getting the gear working because the gear was so shit. They'd had these custom-built desks which were really difficult to work on and they weren't very good quality. Which is why C.G.S. came in, they put in a £100K Neve console.

So, I put the tape to one side. I didn't get uptight about it because there was nothing to get uptight about, bands come and bands go. Then I bumped into Brian once, doing one of those Sunday walks around the Science Museum. Much to my surprise he said "Oh hi, how are you doing?". I didn't think he would recognise me. Then time just went by, I was very busy doing my stuff. I did all sorts of stuff, Renaissance albums, I had a single out with Ringo Records...

Did you meet Ringo?

Oh, aye, yes.

What was he like?

Lovely! This must have been 1975, whatever year Queen did the Christmas simulcast concert. I had a concept album, a Sci Fi based thing, called 'House Up in the Stars', which I was knocking on doors for. I managed to get an appointment at Ringo Records. I didn't think I'd be seeing Ringo Starr, I just thought it would be some bloke. So, I got the address and it turns out it was a wee side door besides Barclay Brothers' Rolls Royce showroom in Berkley Square. I went up the steps, into this wee office, probably worth millions now, as you can imagine. I walked in and sitting at a table was Ringo Starr and Harry Nilsson. They were having a cup of tea and they said "Hello, fancy a cup of tea?". So, Harry Nilsson makes me a cup of tea, we just had a chat and it was all very friendly. I played him a couple of tunes from the concept album, on a big open Revox. He said, "That's a bit of fun but it's not really for us, we're just very small". I think whilst Ringo Records lasted, they only did something like twelve records. He said, "I'm sorry about that, what else have you got?". I said, "I've got this rather daft Christmas thing I've been doing, just for a giggle". He said "Put it on then…".

Basically, it was a rocked up version of 'Away In A Manger' with some friends of mine from Principal Edwards Magic Theatre. He said, "That's a bit of a giggle. I'll give you £400 advance, we'll put it out". I thought, "That's bloody fantastic!". It was the first time I'd ever earned any money from a tune, as you can imagine.

By that time, I was working as an engineer at CBS Records in Soho, it was only a ten-minute walk between places and I'd just done this in downtime. So, I used that money to buy a second-hand colour tv, which I then watch Queen's 1975 simulcast on.

So, what did you do after that music-wise?

I was fed up with living on the outskirts of London, because you are just one of a million guys. I thought I would go to Edinburgh. It would be interesting. Although I wasn't rich or famous, I could do stuff that people who live up there and work in the music business didn't know how to do, because they hadn't been exposed to the processes. If you've got experience, you should use it. So, I came up to a small recording studio in Edinburgh, I did some downtime music recording with a guy I met who was a songwriter. Now, because my wife was an air stewardess, I could get a return flight to Los Angeles for £60. So, I made a fake album up on a cassette, with some fake artwork. Just a little black and white picture. We called ourselves R.A.F., as an acronym for Rich And Famous. A bit tongue in cheek, you know. It was a little bit Queen, a little bit Foreigner, rock music but produced as pop music, you would say. Looking back now, I guess it was a bit derivative but it was quite decently pro-level. I had a five minute segue that I had made that was basically all the hooks.

So, I went to Los Angeles, got myself a wee room in a motel in Santa Monica, and I hired a car. What I didn't know, when I saw all these addresses of record companies on or around the Sunset Strip, I didn't know it was 47 miles long!

I made a few telephone appointments and knocked on a lot of doors. The pitch was, "Hi, I've come 6,000 miles, I've got a five minute segue, come on". You'd be amazed how often it worked. I got shown the door in most places, admittedly but A&M Records liked it. So I actually got an album deal out of that. The reason for me telling you all that, it brings us to the next minor Queen thing...

We booked ourselves a month in AIR Studios, Studio Two. I had the album as demos but I had to recreate it in full quality. As you can imagine, I never really told anyone at A&M that I'd been in Queen because by that time they were big. We're talking about 1978, 79, I suppose. So, I never really traded on it because for me, there was an element of failure, it wasn't a success for me, you know? I mean, I didn't hate the guys, if anything I hated myself for not being simpatico enough to be the right person.

It was great being at AIR Studios, bearing in mind that by now I had been a professional recording engineer for some years and I knew quite a lot of people. So, I was walking down the hallway, it's twelve o'clock at night and I'm about to do some dubs. I was bumping into Lyndsey De Paul, who I hadn't seen in two years and all sorts of people.

At that time, Brian May was doing some work on The Concert for Kampuchea. He was in one of the mixing rooms, which were great at AIR because the mixing rooms were really quite small studios, probably only 3x4 metres. The entire width was a sodding great Neve console, complete with flying faders, that whizzed up and down like bloody magic. So, I'm walking along the corridor and I bump into Brian. Much to his credit, he said, "Oh hi! How are you doing?". I said, "I'm doing fine, thank you very much. I'm doing an album here". Brian said, "Oh that's nice". So, I said, "If you have got ten seconds, would you do me the honour of saying hello to the guys? They'd be knocked out". He said, "Yeah, alright!". Obviously through a bit of chat, these guys knew that at one time in the distant past, I had been in Queen. But sometimes, bearing in mind that we were 450 miles from London, there was no evidence. Was it just a story I used to tell from my days in bands in the Smoke? So we were in Studio Two at AIR, it was a beautiful room, surrounded by windows looking down onto Oxford Circus. I've got the guy who runs A&M's A&R as our producer, David Kershenbaum. He and the guys were sitting around. I walked in, and from behind me walks Brian May. I said, "Hi guys, I just bumped into Brian and he wanted to say hello!". If you could have seen so many jaws hitting the fucking desk, it was great! That was quite a nice moment. It was like, "You see? I wasn't lying!" [laughs]

Can we hear the R.A.F. material online? Is it on YouTube or anything?

Not really. But some of it is quite interesting. The second album, because it was 1980, we were trying to be a bit different. When we were gigging with that, we did a gig at the Marquee. Which was where Jethro Tull found our keyboard player and pinched him! But he was very good... So, for a period of time, I was that professional guy with a band, made two albums and came out of it without owing anybody any money.

Just as an observation with the stuff I've seen online, Queen fans seemed to have really taken you to their hearts.

I have to say, it's been very nice. There have certainly been a few people who have been well intentioned and very pleasant and that is very nice. I have enjoyed that, yes. That's one of the reasons I have been motivated to help out at the conventions.

What sort of music do you enjoy listening to these days?

The most played music in my car is Steely Dan. They have got some cracking songs. They are a little bit jazzy in some respects, you have to think of the time they were made. In the same way that Led Zeppelin would have strange and slightly weird medieval word links to things, there are word links in their songs that take you in different directions. They're very good. Basically two guys, making albums to the best of their ability with the best musicians they could find.

I've still got Cream's 'Disraeli Gears', Led Zep's 'I' & 'II', all those. Because I worked in recording studios the biggest folder in my car player is 'miscellaneous' and that's got 30% classical music, 5% Jazz and mostly a collection of middle of the road, veering towards rock, pop music. I never liked rap. The only thing close to rap I ever liked was John Cooper Clarke in the '70s. I loved his cassettes. So, yes it's a mixed bag but good pop music is good pop music, it doesn't matter who made it.

Doug Bogie was speaking to David Geldard.

Admiring Queen... From The Other Side Of The World

Chris Lee

Born in the right vintage but wrong geographical location, that is how I often describe myself.

Growing up in Malaysia, a tiny country in Southeast Asia 10,576 km away from the United Kingdom, it was not easy to be a Queen fan. Back then, before we knew anything about Google, YouTube and social media, I had to totally depend on vinyls, books and magazines which arrived on our shores months after publication, if at all. Our local English radio station had a Rock Hour programme which almost always ignored Queen and played other rock bands instead, the likes of Deep Purple, Led Zeppelin, The Rolling Stones, Aerosmith and of course The Beatles. It would indeed be a blue moon night when/if I heard Queen over the airwaves.

Why the obsession with Queen? I was given the 'Sheer Heart Attack' LP as a birthday present by an uncle who visited the UK. One spin of the vinyl and I was hooked. 'Killer Queen', in particular, fascinated me tremendously with its unusual lyrics, Freddie's spirited singing and the band's great harmonising. Just as the song suggested, my mind was duly blown into smithereens by the dynamite with laser beam. It was love at first spin. Prior to this, I had heard some recorded songs from their debut album (courtesy of the same uncle, bless his soul!) but silly me wasn't too impressed then. 'SHA' opened my eyes and truly convinced me that Queen was the genuine article, not some run-of-the-mill rock band-wannabe. The whole album was a glorious showcase of what the band was capable of – a rip-roaring ride from 'Brighton Rock' to 'In the Lap of the Gods... Revisited', with classics like 'Tenement Funster' and 'Stone Cold Crazy' thrown in for good measure – what an eclectic mix of goodies packed into one single album!

My heart was instantly captured. By the four young musicians who complemented one another so amazingly. By Roger in particular, that talented and ridiculously good-looking drummer from a rock n roll band. A perfectly natural reaction for a 17-year-old girl then, little did I know that the attraction would persist over the decades right to my sixties (and most likely beyond). Roger has certainly aged well. I love his looks then and now. I love his music, his incisive interviews, his philosophy and outlook in life. But then I digress…

Since my eureka moment with 'SHA', Queen became my number one band, which was not a popular choice as Queen was so low profile in my country. It meant anxiously waiting for their albums to reach our shores months after the UK release, and having to be contented with admiring them from afar. Concerts were obviously out of the question for me. At that time it would be unthinkable (not to mention economically unfeasible) for a teenager to travel overseas for Queen concerts in various parts of the world, not even Japan. I would dream of myself being among the crowd and watching these gorgeous boys in action, but it remained an unattainable dream. What I need right now is a time machine to transport me back to the glorious

70s, so that I can experience first-hand those heady days of Queen playing in live gigs.

Admittedly, the focus had not always been on Queen all this while, particularly during those depressing years after Freddie's passing. Career, postgraduate studies, marriage and raising a family with young kids put paid to that. But my interest was reignited with the advent of the internet, and especially after joining Facebook Queen groups and getting to know many like-minded fans. It is so much easier to follow Queen nowadays. Everything is accessible at a click of the mouse – music, interviews, documentaries, and of course the various social media platforms. It has also become my favourite pastime. Many happy hours have been spent getting lost in their music and falling deeper and deeper in love with the boys. It is a wonder that none of their music sounds dated even though some have been written and performed almost 50 years ago. Some songs – 'Is This The World We Created', 'These Are The Days Of Our Lives' just to name two – are as relevant today as when they were written in 1984 and 1991 respectively. Queen's music is simply ageless and timeless… Still so good after all these years.

On 23 February 2020, right before the world turned crazy with the COVID-19 pandemic, I managed to fly to Perth, Australia, for the QAL Rhapsody Tour. It was a surreal experience to be finally watching my idols in action. I was almost in tears when Roger played the drums and sang 'I'm In Love With My Car'. Finally my dream was fulfilled, a dream that I had harboured since 1975. It was a whirlwind trip just to watch Roger, Brian and the ensemble in action. Two weeks after I returned from Perth, my country went into a total lockdown as we felt the full force of the pandemic. Talk about fortuitous timing!

My sole concert experience was obviously nothing compared to those who had the good fortune of watching Freddie and the gang strut their stuff during their prime, and people can bitch about Adam Lambert for all I care. For me, myself, from my little corner of the world, it was a magical and emotional experience, something which I will cherish until the day I die. This will probably be my one and only Queen+ concert featuring Taylor. My head tells me that once is enough, but my heart tells me to go for the Rhapsody Tour UK/Europe 2022. Not sure if my head or my heart will win the battle in the end… Any way the wind blows….

In the Lap of the Pods Interview

Paul Moody, David Moody and Joe McGlynn are the hosts of In the Lap of the Pods, *a podcast which casts an honest and critical ear over the work of Queen.*

How did the podcast begin?

David Moody: The podcast is just over a year old, we started it during lockdown. It actually started off because we were listening to another podcast that was discussing Freddie. There was a lot of real inaccuracies. I guess, jumping to conclusions about what had happened in certain periods in Freddie's life. We were having a chat in our WhatsApp group about it and I think it was Paul who said, "Why don't we do our own podcast?". So in that moment, we said, "Let's give it a go. Next Saturday, let's record it". It's interesting, I was listening to the first podcast earlier today, just to see how different it is now. It was very much three guys who are pretty nervous and didn't know what they are doing! That was it though, it was just to share our love of Queen. Not to say that our opinion is the only opinion, it's just our opinion. We're coming from a particular angle. That's the thing though, you have Queen fans from more of the rock/metal side of things, Queen fans who come from the pure pop side, you have Queen fans from the early seventies 'prog' side. There's so many different angles you can have with Queen, because of the diversity of the music. It's not like it's an AC/DC podcast. No disrespect to AC/DC, because they're great, but if you said, "Ok we're going to talk about their next album", you're probably going to end up saying the same things you said about the last one. But, y'know, AC/DC are fucking great!

Absolutely! I love them!

Joe McGlynn: Absolutely, aye!

David: In terms of how we met, Paul is my older brother. He's the one that got me into Queen. He bought 'A Night at the Opera' and just hearing him play that album, also 'Greatest Hits' and the Montreal video ['We Will Rock You', originally released on VHS in 1984, then re-released on DVD/Blu-ray as 'Queen Rock Montreal' in 2007], I just got stuck in. I actually met Joe at school. We actually started talking a week after Freddie died. He was already a big Queen fan.

Paul Moody: As David said, I bought 'A Night at the Opera'. It was the first LP that I ever bought. The reason I bought it was because we have an uncle who is really into music, Black Sabbath, Rush, Rory Gallagher, etc. He had a cassette copy of 'Greatest Hits'. I stuck it on, track 1 – 'Bohemian Rhapsody'. That's it, you're away, you know, into this amazing world! So, it started from 'Greatest Hits'. I then bought 'A Night at the Opera' and then all the albums and music I could get. We used to rent the 'We Will Rock You' video from the video store. I think we were the only ones who ever rented it! I think if we had kept it the guy at the video store wouldn't have cared, you know? Just watching that Montreal gig, it was just incredible and falling in love with Freddie and his moves. So, from then on, that was it... under the spell!

Joe: My story with Queen started when my Dad bought me 'Greatest Hits' and Paul McCartney's greatest hits ['All the Best']. I remember sitting in the back of my Dad's Austin Allegro, I was young but I think it was around 1986, '87? My Dad, being a Glaswegian, threw me this bag. "There's your birthday!" The bag had two tapes and a Walkman in it. My Dad said, "Put that one on first!", pointing to the Paul McCartney one. I remember putting it in, playing a little bit of it and just thinking, "meh!". I put the Queen tape in and [clicks fingers] it was just right away, "What is THIS?!". I was just obsessed with them. I remember taking the tape home to my brother Gary, who is around the same age as Paul, just that bit older than me and I said, "My Dad got me this for my birthday!". Gary put it on and he was instantly hooked as well. With him being older, like Paul, he just went crazy and bought everything. In a very short period of time, he just went out and bought the entire back catalogue. So, in the late eighties, he was just obsessed with Queen. He got The Cross albums, he even got the Smile album and this was in 1989! I was absolutely blown away by the band and seeing the 'We Will Rock You/Montreal' video, I was just obsessed with the band and with Freddie, even though I hadn't met David and Paul at that point. To this day, it's still the music that moves me the most, without a doubt. Queen were like my gateway band to heavy rock and ultimately, metal. They are THE most important band for me.

It's funny how Queen span so many genres of music. You get Metallica fans that like Queen. You get Madonna fans that like Queen. There are Andrew Lloyd Webber fans that like Queen. I think there are lots of us that are fans of heavy rock, because of Queen.

Joe: Absolutely! One hundred percent! Being into Queen also makes you get into other types of music. Say, for example, you had just got into Black Sabbath. Then you would probably be blinkered, you know, just into the heavy stuff. I always gravitated to the heavier side of Queen but I still loved the lighter stuff. It made me appreciate the lighter side of music as well as the heavier stuff. Queen made you open minded to like other music outside of of heavy stuff too.

Paul: I think when you've got a band like that, it sets you up for life.

Joe: Aye, the diversity is a really healthy situation for music in general.

I live not too far away from Castle Donington and I've been to eight of the last ten Download Festivals. It's weird how much the heavy genre has diversified and not just in the music itself, either. I've seen guys at that festival in drag, I've seen guys dressed as crayons, a guy dressed as a Tellytubby. You can be anyone, dressed anyway you like at a rock & metal festival now. Back in the 'Monsters of Rock' days, you would have probably have been lynched for wearing any other than the traditional denim or leather with sew-on patches.

Paul: I think two bands who kind of heralded the Nu-Metal thing, who brought metal into the modern age were Nine Inch Nails and Faith No More. The members of which are Queen fans. So, Queen absolutely had a hand in it.

Joe: Faith No More are a band that, for me, draw comparisons to Queen quite a lot. In the sense that every song is different on the record. It can go from something like lounge music to something that is just thrash-y with Mike Patton screaming.

I agree with that totally, I am a big Faith No More fan, I love them. Now, if I could ask each one of you, do you have a favourite Queen album?

David: Don't ask me a favourite because I have FIVE favourites! [laughs] My favourites are 'Queen II', 'Sheer Heart Attack', 'News of the World', 'The Game' and 'Innuendo'. They are always the albums that resonated with me.

'Queen II' because of the absolutely amazing musicianship, the actual song arrangements that are on that album. Just phenomenal. 'March Of The Black Queen', 'Father To Son' [the opening song], there's lots of heavy metal on that album, there's folk music on there, 'Someday One Day' is very earthy. You have the swagger of Roger on 'Loser In the End'. On the first album there was a glimmer of greatness but on the second album they knew exactly where they were going.

'Sheer Heart Attack', that was the album where you thought, okay, they are not going to just stay within the rock perimeter: they are going to move beyond that. Songs like 'Bring Back Leroy Brown'... that's insane how they were able to do something that good. They were able to mimic those styles that came before and do it to a tee. Then, of course, you've got 'Killer Queen', which is their first real pop song and what a song! There's a real diversity on 'Sheer Heart Attack'.

'News of the World': There were lots of styles on 'A Night At The Opera' and 'A Day At The Races', which are great albums, but it's Queen coming out of the other end of that and thinking "strip it back" and let's get back to basics a little bit. There's not a lot of harmonies on it, it's just, "let's reset a little bit" and they went back to their roots on that one. It's a very stripped down album and I love that.

'The Game': Again, it's stripped back. It feels like an album where they went back to their childhood a little bit, a bit of rock n' roll, 'Crazy Little Thing'... it was like they were re-tracing their teenage years and the music they grew up with. There are some amazing tracks, 'Save Me' is a beautiful ballad. The vocals on 'Rock It (Prime Jive)'... just fucking amazing, man!

'Innuendo': There's an emotional connection to 'Innuendo' that most Queen fans, who were fans at the time of its release, will have. Whether it's because the music is great or because of the time it was recorded, with what was going on [with Freddie]. The title track is one of my favourite tracks. It's an absolutely amazing piece of music. The fact that they were able to do that so late in their career was just so impressive. It harked back to 'Queen II' or maybe 'A Night at the Opera'. To still have the chops and the interest to be able to create something like that, is really something. 'The Show Must Go On'... Freddie's vocals and Brian's lyrics come together, it's just beautiful. The album is not without it's flaws, there's a few things on it that could have been different, but as a whole, as an album it was a fitting way to say goodbye to Freddie. So those are my five, sorry, I can't pick just one!

Paul: The best album Queen have ever done is 'Queen II'. It's just perfect. My favourite album however, is 'A Night at the Opera'. It's mainly because it was the first LP I ever bought. It's got lots of sentimental meaning for me. It's something

I'll stick on when maybe things in my life aren't going great because it's something familiar and warm, so it's a very important album for me in that respect.

Joe: This is hard for me. From the first album, 'Queen' to 'The Game', it's a flawless catalogue of music really. I include 'Jazz' in that. I know the other two guys aren't really into that album but 'Jazz' is an important album for me because when I was young, my brother used to play it a lot. Saying that, it's got to be 'News of the World' for me. That's my favourite Queen album and probably my favourite album of all time. I can't actually pinpoint why. I don't know why that album is my favourite, it's just it's a wee bit more important than the rest, for me. Having said that, I fucking love all the songs on it. I think every member of that band wrote a masterpiece on that album, that maybe they didn't on every one of their other albums. 'It's Late' is one of my favourite Queen songs. 'Sheer Heart Attack', again, is one of my favourite Queen songs. People might laugh at me for that but that got me into extreme music. I was like, "What is THIS?!", that was the most heavy thing I'd heard at that time. 'Spread Your Wings', John's song, is one of my favourites. Freddie's 'Get Down, Make Love' and 'We are the Champions'. That album, for me, was Queen at the absolute pinnacle of their songwriting. I love the sound of that record, it's just so warm. I just love how weighty the whole album is, very organic, very stripped back, like David said.

It's interesting what you were saying there, about the song 'Sheer Heart Attack'. Queen were very clever and at that time the musical landscape was changing with punk. 'Sheer Heart Attack' for me, out-punks punk!

Joe: It's actually verging on hardcore punk! It's much faster than anything The Sex Pistols ever did, it's faster than The Ramones!

Seeing as none of you guys ever got to see Queen live, do you have a favourite Queen concert either from videos, live albums or bootlegs?

Joe: 'We Will Rock You', Montreal 1981 for me, hands down.

David: Montreal, absolutely. Another one that sticks in my head is the Houston gig from 1977. It was professionally filmed but it's not been officially released. Freddie was wearing catsuits at that time and Texas wasn't probably the easiest place to do that [laughs] but they were like, "Yeah, we're flamboyant but we'll rip your face off!". They were ferocious at that time. They would've easily demolished any band, they were so heavy and aggressive. If you'd have put them against Black Sabbath or Judas Priest or Zeppelin, Queen would've sounded like Carcass by comparison [laughs].

What about their solo records, do you have any favourites?

Paul: 'Fun In Space' by Roger Taylor.

Joe: I second that. 'Fun In Space' is by far my favourite Queen solo record.

David: I'm going to be boring and say 'Fun In Space' too!

Paul: The first one was also the best one!

Joe: It was better than some Queen records in my opinion.

That album has a couple of famous fans. I know that Def Leppard's Joe Elliott loves that album, he often plays 'Magic is Loose' on his radio show. Also, Ginger Wildheart is a fan of that album too. So, getting back to the In The Lap of the Pods podcast, what kind of feedback have you had back?

David: It's been mostly positive. We don't sugar coat it. If it's got to be said, it get's said. We try not to be smug or arsehole-ish about it, we try to sell it as it's just our stand on things. "You might love this track, we don't", that kind of thing. At the end of the day, we're fans, the same as you. The same as anyone else. Just because we do a podcast and some people listen, we don't put ourselves on a pedestal. We're no different than any other Queen fan, you know? They are allowed to have their opinions on albums and songs in the same way we do. So, the feedback has been mostly positive. We did a podcast on the 'Made In Heaven' album and we gave our thoughts on that. It was very scathing at points and we try and be as fair as we can. Some fans see that as the jewel in the Queen catalogue. Again, cool, if that's what you think. I think a few people were like, "Jeez, you went for the throat here!", but that's ok, that's cool, we invite that. We take their point, it's fine. We're not saying, "This is the only opinion to have and no other opinion exists". We won't fight back with anyone unless it's something exceptionally ridiculous.

Social media guys are fantastic, the fans engage with us on there and talk to us. It's been great. Every couple of weeks there'll be someone saying, "Hi, I'm so and so, I listen to your podcast." We had an email from a lady in New Zealand actually, just last week. I don't know whether she engages with us on social media, but she emailed us and said, "I'm actually going back through all your podcasts again. I love the humour. I'll be out, walking the dog, listening to it and laughing out loud. People are looking at me like I'm strange!" We're blown away by the reaction to it!

Paul Moody, David Moody and Joe McGlynn were speaking with David Geldard.

Growing Up With Queen

Kari van ter Beek

My story starts when I went to see 'Wayne's World' at the cinema. I was 12 and thought the 'song in the car' scene was amazing and I wanted to know more about who originally performed it.

Thanks to my Dad's cassette collection, I was able to discover more of Queen. He didn't have all the albums, and living in a small village outside Aberdeen there wasn't much chance of getting a job to earn money to buy more albums. But luckily, I was able to request them at the local library and borrow them that way. The first ever piece of Queen music I owned was 'Greatest Hits II' on cassette that I received for my thirteenth birthday. I also remember choosing 'The Miracle' on CD for doing really well in a maths class – I am surprised that CD was not burned out from over playing too much!

The problem was, in the '90s at school you could only like Oasis, Blur or Nirvana. Queen was a big no no. In time, I discovered the Queen Fan Club and realised that there were more fans like me out there and I didn't feel too left out.

I attended my first Queen convention in 1998 and met so many nice fans who made me feel so welcome. I took as many photos as I could, even one guy who was dressed as Freddie Mercury – and his name really was Freddie and he came from The Netherlands!

In 2000, I was also invited to the Dutch Queen Day. I didn't want to go at first as I couldn't speak Dutch, but I was told this wasn't an excuse as most people spoke English. I went and not only was it my first Dutch Queen Day, but also my first time in The Netherlands.

Over the years, I have moved house quite a few times, usually because of love! But my Queen collection has always come with me. I've never sold anything from it. I still have all my books that I bought with my pocket money as a teenager – they are very dog-eared as I read them all the time as I wanted to know everything about Queen.

I first visited Montreux and the Freddie Mercury statue in 2004 and was amazed by how beautiful a place it was. I met someone there who I eventually married in 2007.

In 2006, I bought a 'We Will Rock You' musical poster signed by Brian and Roger at the auction at the Queen Convention. It was the first time I really took part in the auction and I was really chuffed to have won this particular item. When I got home, I emailed Ben Elton's management to ask if he would sign it for me as well, so this lovely piece hangs in my hallway and I smile whenever I see it. I also bought a signed 'Return of The Champions' poster in 2011 and this takes pride in my living room.

In 2012, I was in the process of getting divorced. I spoke to a lot of friends who were always there for me, particularly one guy – cue Freddie from The Netherlands! We kept in contact ever since my first convention in 1998 and whenever we met up at the conventions in England or The Netherlands, we would spend ages chatting over drinks. We decided to get together after a few months of chatting every day by text.

Whilst travelling back and forth between the UK and the Netherlands, I landed at Schiphol one day and couldn't see Freddie who had come to meet me. A few seconds later, I saw him frantically waving and shouting, "I just saw Roger Taylor come through arrivals, come quick!" So we walked to where he was standing. I really could not believe he was standing there at the same time I had travelled to the airport! I was ever so polite for some reason. I said, "Excuse me, Mr Taylor? I know it's your private time, but I wondered if I could have a photo with you?" He said he was in a rush, but if it was quick, then it was okay. Unfortunately, the photo was a little blurry, but I was so thrilled to have finally met a member of Queen!

In 2013, I took the plunge and fulfilled my 13-year dream by moving to The Netherlands to be with Freddie. I sold quite a lot of items such as CDs, DVDs, furniture so I didn't bring a lot with me – but, of course, the Queen collection was not sold!

Freddie also has a large Queen collection which he keeps in a 'man cave'. He proposed to me at the Freddie Mercury Birthday party in Switzerland in 2015 and we got married in Scotland in 2017. But somehow, even though we are married, we have never integrated our Queen collections. His collection stays in the man cave, mine is in the spare bedroom on bookcases which also doubles up as my office as I work remotely for a company in Germany, so not a bad place to work in.

I have made so many friends over the years because of Queen. I've never attended a concert on my own, because someone I know will be there.

And at Queen Conventions, it takes a long time to walk from the table you are sitting at to get to the bar because you are guaranteed to meet friends you haven't seen in a while, and before you know it, half the night has gone because you've been chatting to lots of people. I am pretty sure it will be much the same only longer when we finally get together at the next convention when this craziness is over!

I'm not sure where I would be if it hadn't been for Queen. I certainly wouldn't have my own Freddie for sure or have lots of friends to chat to and I don't think I would have ever considered living in a different country. But again, The Netherlands was because of Queen.

I firmly believe the song 'Friends Will Be Friends' was written for all us fans in mind.

Man From Manhattan: The Eddie Howell Interview

Singer-songwriter Eddie Howell's 1976 single 'Man From Manhattan' was produced by Freddie Mercury and features Mercury on piano and backing vocals with Brian May.

How did you became interested in music and who are your influences?

Let's go back to when I was a kid, my Dad used to be a singer, he used to sing and he used to write poems, actually. He was a music fanatic and he used to get some great records. He used to get Louis Armstrong, Count Basie, Duke Ellington, Frank Sinatra, some amazing records! On a Sunday afternoon, he liked to have a drink in his room, where he had a nice record deck and he'd play Sinatra, for instance, and he'd call me, I'd be about 12 years old. He call me, "Ed! Come in here quick!". He'd have a drink in his hand and he'd be playing 'Nancy (With The Laughing Face)' by Sinatra. I don't know whether you know that one? It's a lovely song.

Yes, I do.

He'd stand there saying, "Listen to this bit! Listen to his timing!" He was such an enthusiast. I don't know about you, but when I was a kid, I call always listen to anyone talking about any subject, if they were enthusiastic about it. I love enthusiasts. He encouraged me with music but I didn't like it, because I was a kid. I didn't want to listen to Frank

Sinatra. I'd rather hear 'Rock Around the Clock' or a bit of Elvis.

I remember the first time I really became interested and in love with a piece of music was when I was in a youth club. I suppose I was about 14 years old and through the door of the youth club leader's office came this fucking sound! I couldn't believe it. I thought, "What the hell? What's that?" and of course, it changed my life. It was 'Please Please Me' by The Beatles.

Now you're talking, The Beatles are one of my other great loves!

I got the record; I went to the record shop and bought it for 7/6. I looked on the sleeve and underneath the title 'Please Please Me', it had the composers Lennon & McCartney. I thought, "Lennon & McCartney? They're the band!" because before that, Cliff Richard never used to write his own songs, people were either artists or songwriters. I was fascinated by the fact that they had written this wonderful piece of music. I think that planted a seed; I don't know whether I was conscious of it. I think from that moment, I really wanted to have a go at writing songs. I formed a band soon after that. We played at the youth club. We were called The Wings Of A Bat. Just four Brummie kids. I developed and I started to write my own tunes. The band played my tunes live, that was the bit I'll never forget. They were crappy old songs really; I can't remember any of them now. I carried on and my Dad bought me a little Grundig tape machine and I just used to make little demos, because I couldn't really play guitar but I did my best. I progressed, joined another band, I was writing songs and I thought, "Wow! People actually like them!". I thought there might be something in it.

Then I got married, had a kid and everything stops for a few years, I had to bring home the bacon but I always wanted to fulfil this dream. I was getting more sophisticated with my writing, the guitar playing was coming on and I was playing a little bit of keyboard. I used to make four or five demos of my tunes, pack them up in a little tape box and take a train from Birmingham to London and knock on the doors. I got turned away, as you do, it's difficult to get in anywhere unless you've got an intro, even back then.

I carried on and I left a tape in the Chrysalis Records office, I gave it to the receptionist. I came back to Birmingham and a couple of days later, I had a telegram from Chrysalis Music. They really liked the songs. They'd love to come up to Birmingham and watch a gig if I'm playing. So, we arranged it and four or five Chrysalis people came up. We did the gig and it was like a Simon and Garfunkel type duo I had, just me and a bass player, Joe Pasternack, I was playing acoustic guitar. We played a half hour set. Chrysalis liked it. We went out for dinner that night and talked about deals (which I knew absolutely nothing about). Low and behold, a couple of weeks later, we signed a contract and they gave me an advance, which enabled me to bring my wife and kid to London.

Then I was just writing songs at the Chrysalis studio with other writers. I didn't really get anywhere. I think a couple of Dutch bands did a cover. There was a guy called Nigel Haynes, who was running the publishing company at Chrysalis, told me I should do my own stuff. But I always wanted to be a backroom boy, I never wanted to be a performer really. I was playing in bands so I could highlight my songs. I was never serious about performing because I was too much of an introvert. I never really thought I had a great voice or anything like that, so I stayed with song writing because I loved it. But anyway, he persuaded me. I met a couple of managers, I never really got on too well with them, so he introduced me to somebody called David Minns, who was working at the time with Paul McCartney. He was also managing The Scaffold, who of course had Mike McGear, McCartney's brother. So, I met David and I really liked him. We had a good old chat; we had a lot in common. He loved the music, he wanted to take on the role of managing and get me a recording deal. He got me one in two weeks. The two record companies that were interested were Dark Horse Records (George Harrison's label) and Warner Bros., one of the biggest record companies in the world. I couldn't believe it! In the end, we went with Warners and signed a deal. This was 1975.

So, was it around this time you came into contact with Freddie Mercury?

Well, I made an album, which to this day I'm not very happy with. I'd met a guy called Robin Lumley who worked at Chrysalis, who I became good mates with. He was the keyboard player in a band called Brand X. We'd hired a couple of guys, Gerry Conway on drums, Pat Donaldson on bass. Great players. We were in Trident studios, playing all my songs and I couldn't believe it, it sounded wonderful. Robin Lumley wanted to produce it , so I gave him the job. He was a great keyboard player and a lovely bloke. We got on. So, it was time to get Gerry Conway's drum sound, so Pat Donaldson and I went to the pub for a pint and a pie. We came back about an hour later and he's still trying to get the drum sound. You usually get a drum sound in about ten minutes. Robin came out of the studio and apologised that he couldn't really get the right drum sound for Gerry Conway. I didn't know what was going on. I was a bit naive, just a kid from Brum, really. I thought, "This is a bit strange. He can't get the drum sound? What's all that about?".

So, to cut a long story short, it ended up with Gerry having to leave the studio and Pat did too, they walked out together, to my horror! We'd been rehearsing all morning and it sounded fantastic.

Anyway, they'd left and I though "What are we going to do now?". We'd got two weeks booked to do this album at Trident, we've got a budget but we had no musicians. A couple of minutes went by and the door burst open and in walked Phil Collins, who I'd never met, "Hello Ed!" [laughs] followed by Brand X, Robin's band. So we made the album, they were great players but they were wrong, you know? They were too jazz, too funk. My songs were just delicate little songs. They didn't need too much musicianship, they just needed some sympathetic playing.

So, we made the album and started promoting it. We did a launch for it at a club in Kensington. Warners did a great job, they got everybody down there. There was free booze, free food etc. Phil Collins was playing congas, I was playing guitar, Robin Lumley was playing piano, Jack Lancaster on sax, Ritchie Dharma on drums, Tony Sadler on guitar, it was a great band actually.

We started the set and I think it was about two songs in, I looked over in the dark, onstage and saw my manager David Minns walk in with someone who looked like Freddie Mercury. Of course, it WAS

Freddie Mercury. David had met Fred because he knew John Reid. I thought, "Fucking hell, I've got Phil Collins on my left and I've got Freddie Mercury in front of me, watching me play! What is going on?".

I played 'Man From Manhattan' for the first time at that gig. We hadn't recorded it yet, I'd just recorded it on a little two track tape machine. It was something I'd written after the album but we included it in the set. We got offstage and David came over and introduced me to Fred. He immediately said, "I like that song, 'Man From Manhattan', man". He told me that he would really like to have a go at producing it. He wanted to spread his wings a little bit and have a go at producing.

I wasn't too bowled over by the idea, at first, to be honest. I didn't think my music at the time had anything in common with Queen particularly, I mean I liked what I heard but I didn't know too much about them. I loved 'Killer Queen'. I think 'Killer Queen' is my favourite Queen song. I'll never forget seeing it on 'Top Of The Pops'. Brilliant chords.

So, David was saying, "You've got to fucking do it, man, you're mad, the guys are just about to conquer the world". Fred turned out to be a wonderful character. So, I was more than happy at the time to take the bull by the horns and just do it. I remember I gave Fred my little tape. He called me up a couple of days later and told me to go over to his flat in Holland Road where he was living with Mary Austin. I walked into this flat, it was tiny. In the middle of the room you could hardly move for the grand piano. A huge fucking thing! As I walked in the door Freddie was playing 'Man From Manhattan' and I immediately thought

"Fuck me! He's got it!". It was really nice, a bit fast. I'd always envisaged 'Manhattan' to be a bit like 'Dead End Street' by the Kinks, y'know?

Yes, I can see that.

That was the kind of thing I had in mind when I wrote it.

Yes, it's kind of got that Ray Davies storytelling vibe to it hasn't it? It paints a picture.

Exactly! That's how I heard it, I was thinking saxophones, trombones, etc. But Fred was playing it and it sounded really nice. We did a couple of sessions with it at his place, then we booked the studio, Sarm East it was. By that time, of course, Fred had a chauffeur, he'd made some serious money. The chauffeur used to pick me up in Fulham, where I lived with the Mrs. We used to drive over to Holland Road to pick Fred up. In the back of the car, on the way to Sarm, we had this tiny little cassette machine. Fred was bursting with ideas for the song, he was incredible, I was really impressed. All those backing vocals [sings] "Lot's of moneeeeey", all that suff was on tape. I thought, "Yeah man, that's nice!". Although it wasn't what I envisaged, Ray Davies was nowhere to be seen, but it was going.

So we booked Jerome Rimson, Detroit bass player and Barry De Souza on drums. Barry was a top session player. Jerome was a phenomenal bass player, he played with Aretha Franklin. Freddie knew him from the days of the Sheffield brothers. They were both managed by them.

Didn't Jerome Rimson go on to play with Phil Lynott?

Yes! They were big buddies. Jerome was great. We got to the studio. People in the studio used to look at Fred, because he used to walk into the studio like he was about to go onstage. The rest of us were in jeans and scruffs but Freddie was absolutely immaculate. Everything was sharp.

I think when he sat down at the piano, nobody knew what to expect. He started to play... he was a great piano player, nice feel, he knew his stuff. Eventually we got the backing track down. I remember it became time for my vocal. Freddie said, "Eddie, I think you've really got to go to the top of your range with this". I said, "I am at the top of my range with this, I think I am just about there". He probably thought everyone had a voice like him, he had about twelve octaves! He said, "You've got to do it. All the hit records, even The Beatles, these guys pump it out, they get right up there and make it exciting. I think it would really benefit the song if you just went up a tone". I said, "A tone?!" Fred said, "Come on, try". When he wanted something, Freddie got it. I tried to sing it up there in A. I didn't like it, because I couldn't sing up there.

Then I remember it was Brian May's turn. One morning, we got there at about 11 o'clock. I always remember, the rapport, I saw it immediately. The rapport between Freddie and Brian was something to behold. They really knew, without even saying anything, they knew what to do. Brian didn't even need to think about the solo. He just switched on the tape machine and it was running and Brian played the solo. It was the first take.

That's incredible.

The first take! He knew what he wanted to do, he wanted to do those orchestrated guitar chords, which he did, overdubbed. The rapport between Brian and Freddie, you could almost feel it in the air. There was a great vibe between them.

Brian was nice. I remember talking to him about astronomy. At school, I was always interested in astronomy. I tried to impress him with my knowledge. So, he's listening to me and all of a sudden, he starts to talk. I realised, I was so out of my depth! I couldn't understand what the fuck he was talking about! He was talking about oscillations and black holes... I'm thinking, "Okay...". He was a nice bloke, I got on quite well with Brian.

So, I think we worked for about four days on it, I'm not sure, somebody said it was five. Everyday, I remember, lunch time came and Freddie would get everyone from the studio, even the lowly tape ops, tea makers, about ten of us and march us all down to Brick Lane, which was just around the corner from the studio. That walk from the studio to Brick Lane was ridiculous. Freddie walking down the street, people were just gobsmacked with the way he looked. He had a certain look about him, you couldn't miss him. We got to the Indian restaurant called The Shazam, really posh. We sat there and had what can only be described as a banquet, every day!

I remember looking over at Freddie and thinking, "What a lovely, generous guy!". He was signing the cheque at the end of every meal. I subsequently found out, by the way, as a postscript to this little story, that the generous guy was charging it to my account! [laughs] It was quite amusing.

The experience was quite unforgettable really. I remember how meticulous Fred was in the studio, always in charge. Tom Ruffino [Warner Bros. A&R man] came over from California and went to Sarm Studios because he wanted to meet Fred. Someone came up to the door and said, "Freddie, the Warner Brothers people are here!". Freddie said, "Yes dear! Yes dear! Hold on, we're just in the middle of it". He kept them waiting for two hours and they were paying for it, I couldn't believe it. He kept them waiting because we were busy. Then it was time to let them in. He called them in. They were nice but incredibly sycophantic. Freddie knew how to behave like a star. He knew that these people liked somebody who was like that. He behaved like he was on top of the world, king of the world and that's what they want to see. Freddie had an ego like everybody does but, you know, nothing outrageous.

One of my biggest surprises when I met him was how shy he was. I'd only seen him as this extrovert showman. He was also a generous guy, generous of spirit. I remember the night he asked me if he could produce 'Man From Manhattan' at the club and I said, "Yes!", he took everyone to a restaurant called The Elephant on the River. Kenny Everett was there, I think Roger Taylor was there. The reason why he didn't want to get Roger and John on 'Manhattan', was because he said it would sound too much like Queen. As it was, it did sound like Queen, apart from the main vocal. So, he took us all for this meal. My missus was there. It was all star treatment. Freddie got up and made a toast to me, "This is to Eddie...". It was really nice. So I have got nothing but fond memories of him, you know?

That's lovely.

I was in awe of him, in a way, because he was an incredibly great man, he just was. He was on the case all the time. He genuinely loved that song. He did everything he could to make it work. I'll never forget at the end of the session, I was sitting there in the corner on a little chair in the control room. Mike Stone, who was an engineer on the Queen albums was on the other side of the room and standing there at the front of the desk with his back to me was this person known as Freddie Mercury and I looked at him and I thought, "What the fuck am I doing here, man?" because I'd been living in a caravan in Birmingham a couple of months ago. Freddie turned to me, after it had finished and said, "Eddie, if this is not a hit dear, sue Warner Bros!". I'll never forget that.

So, we finished the record. We recorded in August 1975, I think it was, and I don't think it came out until February, or March maybe of 1976. It did well. We were Record of the Week on Capital Radio. I remember everywhere I went in London, windows were open and you'd hear it blasting out. That was a thrill, hearing your record being played. It was really picking up a load of airplay. David Minns, my manager, had gone to New York with Freddie and the band because they had embarked upon a big tour. I got a call from him, from New York saying, "Eddie, I've got some bad news for you". I said "What?". He said "The Musician's Union have banned 'Manhattan' in the UK. They've put a blanket ban on it". I said, "What?...Why?". He said, "They found out that Jerome Rimson, the bass player, didn't have a work permit". He wasn't a member of the Musician's Union or anything like that.

Now, in those days, the M.U. were really on the side of orchestras, big bands, brass players, musicians. They used to send people looking around the studios for mellotrons and synthesisers. Those two instruments were the biggest enemies of musicians because they took their jobs away. A mellotron could emulate a brass section or an orchestra, a synthesiser could do the same. They used to send people round, scouts, looking for these things, putting a block on them. Rock n' roll, at that time, in the seventies, was like the enemy of the M.U.

I was a member of the M.U. but it didn't make any difference. Warner Bros. called the M.U. up and they had top level meetings at the office in Greek Street. Warners were amazed at time but the M.U. wouldn't budge. So, the record died basically. On the Wednesday, you were walking around Oxford Street and it was blasting out all over the bloody place, two or three times a day you might hear it. Kenny Everett picked up on it, he was just playing it all the time... and then nothing! Ridiculous, it was. I never heard it again on UK radio until years later. So that was the sad end of 'Man From Manhattan' in the UK. Because it was banned, it was Warner's policy never to put a record out in America if it had not become a hit on its own turf. So we missed an opportunity there. So, that's the story of 'Man from Manhattan' in a nutshell.

That was such a shame that such a thing was allowed to happen. It's such a great song, it deserves to be an all time classic, which to me, it is!

That's very kind of you. I wish I could do it again, about a tone lower.

I just love that record. I don't know whether you have ever heard the cover version of it by Valensia?

Yes, that's nice actually! I thought that was well cool. I wrote to him, telling him that I liked it.

There are some good clips of you on YouTube, on a sort of European equivalent of Top Of The Pops.

I saw those, but I don't like watching them! [laughs] It was a great period really, unforgettable.

So, do you still play live Eddie?

I was in a little jazz combo, actually, until quite recently. My girlfriend was the lead singer. We had a great bass player and a violinist called Antonia Boots, who has played all over the world. Great musicians and we just used to do gigs all over London really. One of the nicest gigs I ever did in my life, somebody asked us, because we were doing all these Ella Fitzgerald things, the old 30s, 40s, 50s songs... somebody asked us to play in a hospice. We were just on this tiny little stage and they wheeled the patients in. There was a woman lying in a bed, I'll never forget it. She didn't look like she had long left and the tears were streaming down her face. It was one of the most satisfying gigs I've ever done. Thinking that these people weren't going to be around for much longer and knowing that you could bring a bit of cheer was very nice, you know?

I suppose something like that, where you can see the results of your playing having a response like that, it must feel like magic?

Magic, yes! Absolutely.

Eddie Howell was speaking with David Geldard.

Dear Friends

David Geldard in conversation with schoolfriend and fellow die-hard Queen fan Jon Fowler

Jon, we've been into Queen for such a long time, so many years but can you remember how you first heard them?

I got into them by accident. It was a Thursday or a Friday night in August 1986. My older sister knocked on my bedroom door and said, "Do you want to come to a concert?". I said, "Yes! What is it?". She said, "We are going to see a band called Status Quo. They are playing at Knebworth Park". So, I said, "OK". My sister said, "Unfortunately, I've split up with my boyfriend and we've got a ticket spare". My sister and my auntie were big Status Quo fans. So we jumped into the car, a 1300 Austin Allegro and headed down to Knebworth. I just remember it taking hours and hours to get there. I saw everybody wearing Queen T-Shirts and I said to my sister, "What does that mean?". She said, "They are the main band". You have to remember, I'd just turned twelve years old. I loved the T-Shirt [with the 'A Kind of Magic' cover of the four band members]. I remember it was £5.

We got to the gates and it said, 'No bottles allowed' and we'd just bought two big bottles of Coca Cola, which in those days, I used to drink it like a fish! We had to throw these bottles away because they wouldn't let us in otherwise. So, in we went. I remember Status Quo came on and my sister said, "We've timed this perfectly".

As a kid, I was really into 'The A-Team' and 'Airwolf'. I looked up and saw the helicopter and said to my sister, "Look, it's Airwolf!" and she said, "No, that's the band arriving". I started to get this perception that this was bigger than anything I'd ever experienced in my life.

I remember it was a hot day. I think the entire event must have run out of soft drinks! I recall seeing what I now know was 130,000 people stand up [as Queen came on]. It was like 'Close Encounters of the Third Kind'! The intro to 'One Vision' came on and believe me, it was loud, considering we were about a mile away from the stage. I was just awestruck! I couldn't speak, I was terrified to be honest with you. When they came onstage, that was it. They were just absolutely sensational. That night, I was just quizzing my sister and auntie about Queen on the way back. I was just obsessed with them straight away. I think they just got fed up with me asking questions because they weren't Queen fans, they were Status Quo fans.

So, you got back from the gig and how did your love of the band manifest itself?

It was difficult with very little pocket money to buy a Queen album. Bizarrely, in 1986, it seemed far easier for me to find Freddie Mercury solo stuff. I think maybe my first fifteen purchases were of Freddie Mercury solo stuff. I adored the Freddie Mercury stuff. Then slowly, but surely, friends and family said, "I've got a Queen album" and I'd say, "Can I borrow it?". I remember borrowing 'Live Killers' and 'The Game'. My sister bought 'A Kind of Magic' and she lent me that. But really, my next step to fandom was Freddie's solo stuff, believe it or not. I played the 'A' sides, the 'B' sides, the album 'Mr. Bad Guy' on tape, I played them to death!

I remember somebody giving me eight pounds. I got on my bike to Manchester City Centre, I left it unlocked outside the Arndale and there was a record shop, right in the centre of the Arndale. I picked up a copy of 'The Game' and bought it for exactly eight quid. I went out and my bike was still there. Different times!

We went to primary school together and then went to different secondary schools. Can you remember the day we met up again and bonded over our love of Queen?

Yes! I was having a teenage argument with a friend of mine who was a Michael Jackson fan! I mean, Michael Jackson was big. What a great musician. You might relate to this, but if you were a Queen fan at school in the '80s, some people would try to take the piss out of you and I would defend Queen like crazy, like they were family. I wouldn't have a word said against them. So, me and this friend were having an argument who was the greatest, Michael Jackson or Queen. Then you walked past! I said to my mate, "I'll tell you what, Dave is an old mate of mine. Whatever Dave says will settle this argument because I'm sick of having this argument about who's better. Dave will settle this argument once and for all".

I shouted to you, "Dave! Just off the top of your head, just be honest, who is better, Queen or Michael Jackson?" You stopped in your tracks and said "You're joking aren't you? QUEEN!!!".

You see, in my school, in the eighties, kids were into UB40, Milli Vanilli or whatever was at number one that week. So, they would take the piss out of the fact I was so dedicated to Queen. I could never understand that. Even in 1986, the back catalogue that Queen had was unrivalled. It didn't help that they hadn't released any new material as a band in 1987 or '88. People would say "Oh, they've spilt up haven't they?"

Do you remember those early days of us swapping Queen albums and videos with each other?

Yes! That's what it was like in those days. No internet or mobile phones, nothing like that. I think I came and knocked on your door and said, "Do you mind lending me what you've got and I'll lend you what I've got?". We started trading that way. Some of the stuff you had that I didn't was just amazing and vice versa. It was such a different world then, with no internet. You can just type into YouTube now and listen to anything.

I remember coming around to your house, around 1988 and you said "Look what I've just got!". It was a bootleg tape of the Manchester Maine Road concert from 1986, the Magic Tour. I'd never even heard of bootlegs before!

Yes, you're right. I bought the Maine Road gig on cassette. I've only got tape two these days, tape one has vanished, but it's still the best recording of that gig that I've heard.

So, out of the whole Queen catalogue, what is your favourite album?

'Queen II'. If you ask anyone why 'Queen II' is their favourite album, you would get a different answer every time. It's so complex, so different, it's got absolutely everything on it. To this day, all these years later, I still don't know what it's all about. The very fact that I've not sussed it out is the reason I keep going back to it. Every time I listen to it, I hear something different. It's almost like the record changes slightly every time I listen to it.

It's got so much on there, the overdubs, the changes, the switches, the lyrics, they just take you to a different place. There is no other album that has ever done that too me. I feel the same way about the album today as the first time I heard it.

Do you have a favourite song on it?

I would probably say 'Ogre Battle'. Or maybe 'White Queen'. There's no definitive answer to why I adore 'Queen II'. I just adore that album. It's phenomenal. Don't get me wrong, I love all the other albums, just not as much as that one.

Like me, you are a staunch defender of the 'Hot Space' album...

I love it. Bizarrely, the first Queen single I ever bought was 'Las Palabras D'Amor', which obviously is from 'Hot Space'. When you think about it, 'Put Out the Fire'... what a great track! I always think if they had put that one out as a single, it would have gone top ten. For obvious reasons they got it so right with 'Under Pressure'. There are such great tracks, 'Cool Cat' for example...

I love 'Cool Cat'!

Yeah, you know? I can't put my finger on why people don't like that album. I actually prefer it to 'Jazz' but honestly, I don't dislike any Queen album.

I remember 'The Works' was the first album you bought on compact disc...

...and I absolutely loved it! 'Radio Ga Ga', 'I Want to Break Free', 'Is this the World We Created?',

'Hammer to Fall', it's an outstanding album. It's got everything. It was another 'Queen switch'. The electronic/synthesiser era was in full effect. It was so diverse, you have the anthems, the heavy rock tracks, the electronic stuff like 'Machines (Back to Humans)'. There was only Queen who could do an album like that and get away with it.

Over the years, you have amassed quite a collection of Queen stuff. Thinking back to our teens, I think you were spending every penny you earned on Queen?

From the age of 14, I spent every penny on Queen. I couldn't get enough of them. At 15, I went and bought a hi-fi on finance, so I could play it all, because at that time they had started putting things out on compact disc. Yes, I have spent thousands over the years! [laughs]

I remember you getting so excited about the release of 'The Miracle'.

I love that album. A true return to form. In hindsight, I wish I had understood the title. It was a miracle that it ever got put out. It was nearly called 'The Invisible Men'. I'm glad it wasn't.

I remember the summer that album came out, 1989, was so hot. You'd be out and 'Breakthru' was blaring out of every car window!

[laughs] Yes! That's right!

...and then we got my all time favourite, 'Innuendo'.

Yep, it's Queen's swansong as far as I'm concerned. I know that 'Made in Heaven' was the last album but I regard 'Innuendo' as the last proper album.

Aside from 'Queen II', there's nothing can touch it. What an album.

I remember, like the rest of us, you were deeply upset when Freddie passed away.

It was the Monday morning when we found out wasn't it? Let's not beat around the bush, the fans had known for a long time that something wasn't right. I remember about 3 or 4 that morning I was up. I decided to go downstairs and have a look what was on TV. One of the things I would look at on satellite TV in those days was channels like RTL4 or ZDF. I put the teletext news on and the only thing I could translate was 'Freddie Mercury' but I knew, straight away. I knew he'd gone. In those days you would have to wait until TV-am to come on for the UK news. I thought I'd go to bed and hope that when I wake up, it's not true. I think it was about 8 o'clock the next morning, my Mum woke me up and said, "Do you know?". That was it.

A few months later, we went to the 'Freddie Mercury Tribute Concert'.

What a day that was. I remember your Dad, looking after us. I have memories of the coach driver playing the Leeds 1982 bootleg on the way down to Wembley. I can recall discussions on the coach, what we thought the first song was going to be. Whether there was going to be a 'laser effect' of Freddie on the stage [there had been rumours in the newspapers], we just didn't know. I think there may have been still some of the artists unannounced? We were talking about Montserrat Caballe appearing, Michael Jackson, Madonna, those were the rumours on the coach.

I remember being stood in the queue outside Wembley and the crowds of people! The electricity in the air was unbelievable. Even halfway through the concert though, I still expected Freddie to run out on stage.

We just didn't know what to expect but what we saw that day… was unreal. I know Live Aid was big and had some fantastic acts but, for me, nothing had matched the 'Freddie Mercury Tribute Concert', before or after. You will not see that again.

I was concerned at first [on the day] because we didn't know that the show had been split into two halves. I thought that people watching at home would switch off because they wanted Queen songs. I thought, they probably didn't switch on to watch Metallica play 'Enter Sandman' or Def Leppard playing 'Animal'. Now though, I would give you a million dollars to go back and watch those bands playing those songs. That being said , people didn't switch off, they watched the full thing.

Extreme, in my opinion, did what the fans in the audience wanted. They did a Queen set that was absolutely phenomenal. They did it their own way. It was fans onstage playing to fans in the audience. Extreme knew what we wanted.

The second half, when Brian, Roger and John came on to 'Tie Your Mother Down', that was the point where I really felt like Freddie was going to run out onstage. I felt that was really brave of them, to do that. When you look back, they were the biggest band on the planet. I remember looking at you and thinking, "This is it Dave, we're here!".

Brian started singing and I thought he sounded even better in the stadium than he did on TV or on the Blu-ray. I remember thinking that Queen were going to carry on with Brian as the singer. Later on, after the concert when we'd heard George Michael, I remember us saying that George should join them. People think that George Michael performance is brilliant now, but in the stadium, it was actually ten times better.

For me, the first half had been amazing, because other than Queen, they were all my favourite bands. Particularly Def Leppard. Then when the second half commenced and Queen came on, straight into 'Tie Your Mother Down', for the first time I was seeing the members of Queen together in real life after being such a huge fan for years. I was trying to process that because that moment, being in the crowd, was so exciting. Then, Joe Elliott, my second favourite singer after Freddie, joined them on the song. Not only that but then Slash joins them. My excitement levels were through the roof!

Yes! Joe Elliott was just something else! Then Slash! Then after that Roger Daltrey! And Tony Iommi! It was just an avalanche of the greatest musicians, one after the other. Respect to Queen, they didn't even give us time to get our breath back!

One of the other highlights for me was the David Bowie–Mick Ronson–Mott the Hoople bit, that was incredible. Elton John and Axl Rose doing Bohemian Rhapsody.

Of course, George Michael came on and did ''39' and 'Somebody to Love', which was just extraordinary.

It was amazing, because at the time, we didn't know George Michael was a Queen fan. We considered him to be more pop than rock. So, for him to come on and do "39", an album track from 'A Night at the Opera', that was quite a surprise. That, to me, proved he was a real fan.

Yes, absolutely. We didn't know much about him in those days but then we found out that he used to busk "39" on the London Underground. Nobody knew at the time, but George was also singing for his lover who had been diagnosed with AIDS, as well as singing for Freddie, so the greatest of respect to him.

Even Liza Minnelli, though. The hairs on the back of my neck stood up when Liza Minnelli came on. I'm not saying she was the best but it was the very fact that Freddie would have loved that.

In the years following the Freddie Mercury Tribute Concert, we went to Brian May and Roger Taylor solo shows, what are your memories of those?

Those were great fun! We saw Brian May at the Manchester Apollo in 1993 and 1998 and Roger Taylor at Manchester University in 1994 and 1999.

That first Brian May tour, with Cozy Powell, Spike Edney, Neil Murray, Jamie Moses, Cathy Porter, Shelly Preston... that was an amazing combination. It was the first time that we'd heard Brian sing properly. Brian had released 'Back to the Light' and as a solo artist, he held his own, he was brilliant. He could sing, he could play that guitar, the band was fantastic. He lifted the roof off the Apollo! I remember the crowd response to 'Love Of My Life', Brian looked so emotional. When we saw Roger Taylor at the University, it felt like he was playing in your bedroom for you.

Well, in comparison to the likes of Wembley Stadium or Knebworth Park, it did feel like that. But to see him perform in such an intimate venue was amazing. We were stood right in front of him.

It was thrilling. They'd always claimed they were four equal people, by this stage they'd proved to us they were. By God, Roger and Brian proved themselves on those tours. It was surreal that we were seeing Roger Taylor at Manchester University. To anyone who didn't understand Queen it would be, "Why are you going to watch the drummer from the band?". They didn't understand that he sung, he played the guitar, he sang whilst drumming and that he wrote so many of the songs.

How would you sum up what Queen mean to you?

Ultimately, I know you love The Beatles as well and you love Def Leppard, David Bowie, etc. I'm the same with other bands, Big Country, Def Leppard. I love Led Zeppelin, The Stones, The Who, Extreme, Thunder... but fucking hell, they don't come close to Queen for me.

I'm just so glad that, today, it seems like the penny has dropped with everyone. I'm more at peace now because it feels like everyone agrees with me. Also, at last it seems that it has finally sunk in over in the USA. Put that in the fucking book! [laughs] It's been a journey and it's still not over. We have Roger bringing out a solo album. They are very clever people, they always know what they're doing. I don't feel like I have to collect everything on multiple formats anymore. I used to get the record, the CD, the tape, the download, the picture disc, etc. The reason I did all that was so they charted higher.

We always defended Queen in any 'best of' arguments or discussions. You see these kids doing reaction videos on Queen and they are clever kids, they get it. They're not idiots, they are geniuses.

Queen Fans - The New Generation

Hannah Dennis

I always loved Queen growing up. As a young child both my father and mother played Queen in the background and we'd sing along to them. Honestly, it was a regular part of my life and it did me the world of good.

As I became a teenager, I began to find my own music taste and as Queen was right in front of me, it was a route I was bound to follow. I admired all the band member's creativity and mental strength.

They dressed up in drag for a music video or covered themselves in Vaseline for an album cover. They never cared what people thought in the process and that was definitely a message I needed as I let my own personality blossom.

When reading Freddie's biography, I found many similarities in both our personalities and honesty. I was very surprised but happy. Now at a moment when hardships overwhelm me, I read a section of his biography that I need, as his biography covers most difficulties in life.

It's reassuring to have someone of a similar view discuss his perception of things. Freddie will always continue to inspire me. He was very strong and talented and I'm lucky to have discovered him when I did, as what he and Queen stood for in general, really instilled values in me others around me couldn't at times.

I have always loved Queen's music. I enjoyed how it kept out of the chaotic environment of politics. As Freddie would say, it wasn't 'Change your life with a Queen song'.

I always enjoyed the peacefulness and lack of controversy in that climate. Of course, they had difficulties in the press and constant questions due to Freddie's sexuality but in all honesty I saw them all as human and the press were harsh to every artist they came across. I'm just glad it didn't get to them.

Queen will always be a massive inspiration to me though and I remember the best compliment I received was, "It's like I'm talking to Freddie Mercury!". I hope I can grow to be a better person as I keep on finding out more about them. For anyone who wants to know more about Queen and wants to research them, I suggest you do it, as it will be worthwhile.

Friends Will Be Friends Will Be Friends.

Paul Webb

I have many fabulous memories of the band over the years, but this one always stands out for me. This is my account of the video shoot for 'Friends Will Be Friends'. It took place thirty-five years ago, and all I have to go on is my memory and a few photos that I took, so please excuse me if any this is inaccurate in any way. If it is wrong it will only be slightly wrong, there are no lies or exaggerations.

In May 1986 I received a letter from the Queen Fan Club asking if I would be willing to attend the filming of Queen's next video; as if I would say no. Sadly, I no longer have that letter in my collection. I replied to the Fan Club and was sent a ticket/invitation for the filming. This was all done by Royal Mail, no internet or mobile phones back in those days.

The Magic Tour had already been announced and the single 'A Kind of Magic' had been released on 17 March in the UK, so there was much excitement among Queen fans. The new 'A Kind of Magic' LP would not be released until 2 June 1986, so the song we were about to hear was an exclusive for us.

So a 21-year-old me arranged a day off work on Thursday 15 May 1986 and boarded a train to Stonebridge Park Tube Station (not Stonbridge Park as the ticket stated); I lived in East London at the time, so it wasn't a huge journey for me. I arrived at Stonebridge Studios in plenty of time and we were led to a marquee in the grounds of the studio and were all given a packed lunch; the standard sandwich, apple, chocolate bar and carton of fruit juice.

After a while we were led in groups from the marquee to the studio. As we entered the studio we were met with a jaw dropping sight: a stage and lighting rig which were scaled down versions of those going to tour Europe in the summer, including the zigzag thingummies over the stage, albeit slightly smaller. I'm not sure if we were told at the time that this was the Magic Tour stage, or whether this fact came out at a later date. This studio and stage were also where Queen were conducting rehearsals for the Magic Tour.

Once everyone was inside the studio – about a thousand of us – we were told that the new song, 'Friends Will Be Friends', was going to be played over the PA twice so that we could all familiarise ourselves with it, and then the band were going to come on stage. We were specifically told to sing up during the chorus as our voices were going to be recorded and added to the promo video; yep, that's our voices that can be heard on the video from the second chorus onwards.

They played the song a few times and then the band came on stage; my god the cheering and applause was deafening, and went on for ages. Eventually, with no end in sight to the thunderous applause, Freddie came to the front of the stage to calm us down. I had seen Queen live four times prior to this day, but never this close; when Freddie was at the front of the stage he was less than five feet away from me, it was incredible. Without the help of a microphone, Freddie spoke and the audience fell silent, hanging on to his every word and gesture. He reiterated what had already been said about our voices being recorded and told us what to do, finishing his speech with, "Why am I telling you what to do? You know what to do, once the lights come on just be yourselves."

And then the cameras started rolling and the song started. We swayed, we clapped and we sung our hearts out to the song watching every move the band made. At one point during the filming Freddie, Brian and John came off the stage and walked through the audience brushing shoulders with me as they did so. This would have looked great in the finished video with the band (apart from Roger) being so close and interacting with the audience, but it did not go as planned. Freddie, Brian and John were mobbed, no violence, just adoration, but seriously mobbed. So much so that Freddie dropped his microphone and stand, and in the ensuing mêlée, while security and roadies got the band back on stage, the mike and stand were picked up by members of the audience and separated. I saw one fan place the mike in his inside jacket pocket; what a trophy. But sadly for him a member of the security team saw this too, and the mike and stand were quickly retrieved. Footage of this walking through the audience sequence must still be in the archives somewhere and I would love to see it.

We went through the song umpteen times and between takes the band were chatting, smoking and drinking cans of Heineken lager, with Roger randomly throwing drumsticks into the audience until eventually he declared, "I can't throw any more, I'm running out." At one point Freddie asked, "Has anyone got a fag?", which was met with a reply from a member of audience of "You are a fag, Freddie." Brilliant. We're all here to idolise our favourite band and take part in a piece of their history in a once in a lifetime opportunity and some fool has to shout that out. Just proves the point that no matter where you are in the world and no matter what you do, you will always encounter arseholes. In the end John offered Freddie his half-smoked cigarette.

And so the day went on, with us all going through the song over and over again, mostly in its entirety rather than snippets, or playing it up to or from a certain point. Then Freddie upped the ante and boarded a spotlight that was mounted on a crane arm. We sang the song again with Freddie now shining the spotlight on us as he swooped over our heads.

The cover photo of the single was taken by Peter Hince. The band were led off stage and the audience were invited onto the stage for the photo. I made it onto the stairs on the left-hand side of the photo and unbeknownst to me the band were to be lead back onto the stage via a gap next to those stairs. This was my chance. As each member of the band was lead onto the stage, I managed a handshake and a hello with every one of them before they made their way to the front of the stage for the photo to be taken. Sadly only my arm can be seen on the single's cover, but I can be clearly seen in the video a few times.

We were told from the outset that no cameras were allowed, mainly for the fact that any photos taken would reveal the new stage and lighting rig for the forthcoming tour. I'm (sort of) ashamed to say that I sneaked in my old 35mm camera (digital cameras were still a long way off) and snapped off a few photos. Throughout the shoot to my left was a very tall American man – I'm 6'2" and he towered above me – wearing a light-yellow jacket and sunglasses

The filming of the 'Friends Will Be Friends' video, Stonebridge Studios, 15th May 1986. [Photo © P. Webb]

throughout the day. We chatted between takes, I'd love to get in touch with him again.

All in all it was a fabulous, unforgettable day. Despite having seen Queen live in concert previously, this was something completely different. I saw the band relaxed and chatting with the audience, I had an insight into the video-making process and I got to see Queen so close up it was like they were in my own living room.

I remember as we left the studio to make our way home, I passed a Rolls Royce in the studio car park with Harvey Goldsmith sitting in the back chatting away on a carphone... very flash.

Before writing this, I did a bit of research into Stonebridge Studios to see if it was still there or not. Sadly it isn't, the whole area is a building site as shown in the Google Street View and Google Earth photos. It is such a shame that the building where Queen made this video and rehearsed for their most ambitious tour has been destroyed.

But long live the memories!

As It Began: Jim Jenkins Interview

Queen 'superfan' Jim Jenkins has followed Queen from the very beginning and is the co-author (with Jacky Smith, head of the Queen Fan Club) of 'As it Began', the official Queen biography.

Jim Jenkins with Freddie Mercury. [Photo © QueenOnline]

Can you recall the first time you heard Queen?

I can, very much so. It was on Radio Luxembourg. It was Keep Yourself Alive. My friend told me they were going to be playing it. I used to listen to Radio Luxembourg a lot anyway, on 208. I got told "Queen are going to be on tonight!", so I put it on. I was dying to hear this band that one of my friends had seen twice and he was just raving about them. He was saying how good the singer was. So, anyway, the song came on and the intro went on… and on, I thought "It must be an instrumental!" I had never known a song that took so long to get going as that one did. I was just thinking "Oh my God!" I just loved it. I was trying to listen to the singer, the guitars, the drums… it was just superb! I was in bed listening to it, in North Wales. It's a long time ago now!

What was the first Queen gig you attended?

I went to see them support Mott the Hoople but I didn't go to see Mott, I actually went to see Queen.

My friend who had seen them wrote to me. We didn't have a phone, so we used to communicate with people through letters. So, I got a letter from my friend Graham saying Queen were playing Liverpool, supporting Mott the Hoople, and if I couldn't afford the 60p for the ticket he'd buy the ticket for me!

I was in the fourth row (Row D) at the Liverpool Stadium. I remember the intro playing, 'Procession', I'd never seen an intro done like that before. Then this drummer walked on and got behind the drums, then John Deacon, then Brian May. They went straight into 'Father to Son' and this fella walked out...

I 'd never seen anything like him. The only person who he reminded me of, a little bit, was Alice Cooper. They were all dressed in black and white. Freddie had one leg black and one leg white, a black and white top, long hair and painted black fingernails! He started singing "A word in your ear…". My mate said that my jaw just dropped. I just loved that gig. 'Liar' was the one that stood out for me. I had never been affected by a band like I was that night. I didn't want them to finish. When they did finish, I remember they were watching Mott the Hoople and I couldn't take my eyes off them.

In Liverpool Stadium, after the show, they used to sell doughnuts. So, me and my mate said "Let's go and get doughnuts" and next to me, buying one, was Freddie Mercury. My mate was digging in to me, saying "Speak to him! Ask him for his autograph!". But I looked at him and I thought "Nah, I'll give it a miss!" [laughs].

So how did you become friendly with the band?

Pat and Sue the original Queen Fan Club secretaries left and they got a new secretary, Therese Pickard. I had met Queen in Liverpool in 1975 and this was May '76… Therese wanted to write a biography of the band. She was talking to Brian May and Brian said, "We've got this fan in Liverpool, he's been with us since the beginning, he might know a bit. I think his name is Jim".

Therese then contacted all the Jims in the Liverpool area that were in the fan club [laughs]. Of course, back then there were no computers, it was all done by mail. So, I got this letter asking how long had I followed Queen, had I ever met the band? Etc. So I rang her back and said "Yes I've seen them quite a few times and met them all". Therese said, "Would you like to come down to the office? I would like to talk to you about the history of Queen and what you know". I said, "Sure, I'd love to come down". I went down to the office and Brian was there. That's where it all started really, helping Therese with that. I did a bit of research on them, then Roger came down to the office, John, John Reid and then Freddie. That's how I got to know them. Then the Crazy Tour (in 1979), I did most of the gigs on that tour and we did go out with them after the shows, so I got to know them more then.

So, from your point of view, could you describe each of the members of Queen?

Wow, what a question!

John Deacon – quiet, unassuming, funny, business-like, a dark horse, more to him than meets the eye. I felt he never really showed his true character.

Roger Taylor – typical rock n' roll star. He oozes personality. He's got a great memory. I remember him telling me about their very first gig. He remembered that they started with 'Stone Cold Crazy' and after that they did 'Son and Daughter'. He's a hell of a nice guy, he's what I would call a rock n' roller in the true sense of the word.

Brian May – very, very deep. He listens, he takes onboard what you say to him. Very clever. He's really into fandom, he understands fandom. I think it's because he was a big fan of people like The Shadows, he and Roger were fans of The Who and The Beatles.

Brian is very thoughtful and considerate.

And then of course, Freddie Mercury..!

What can you say about Freddie? He was different. It was hard to keep his attention. If you'd got his attention, you knew it didn't work to be sycophantic with him. He didn't like that. Talk to him about things other than Queen and you would have a better conversation with him. He was funny, charming and very clever. He knew exactly what he wanted to do, where he wanted to go. He aimed for it and succeeded. A great man with great ideas. He turned fantasy into reality.

What do you think would surprise people about Freddie?

He had a great knowledge of things that you wouldn't expect him to know of. He was very interested in so many aspects of life. Maybe it was because of his upbringing and where he lived?

I know when he lived in Liverpool, which was only for a few weeks, we dressed up on a Sunday. We had 'Sunday clothes', which you only ever wore on a Sunday. Freddie was really interested in that aspect of life. I think that might surprise people, his interest of others. You probably would expect him to not give a damn, but he really did.

Have you got a personal favourite memory of each band member?

Yes. John Deacon – When we went to Paris to see Queen in 1979, in the mornings we did all the tourist sites until the early afternoon. Then, of course, we would go to the gig to queue up. One day we to the Eiffel Tower, half of us went up and the other half stayed at the bottom. So, when we went down the others said "You're not going to believe this but John Deacon has just gone up with his son". We waited until he came down. He saw us and walked over to us all, we didn't go to him. He said "Thank you so much for coming all the way over from the U.K. to see us, we really appreciate it!". I couldn't believe a member of the band had thanked us for coming. We said "Thank you for the gigs, last night was absolutely incredible!".

John said "Glad you enjoyed it, enjoy the rest of the shows!". I have got other favourite memories but I'll pick that one, that was special.

Roger Taylor. I went to the studio to see them recording and Roger was so friendly. He was amazing with me, explaining to me how the mixing desk worked. He got John to play me a couple of the songs they had recorded. He sat me behind his drumkit, I said "I can't play the drums", so he put the drumsticks in my hand and took my hand to play the drums. So that's my memory of Roger, that's a fun one.

Brian May. My God. Brian, so many memories of Brian.

Brussels, The Game Tour. Me and my mate arrived at the hotel in the morning and Brian was in the foyer. He came over to us and said "Have you eaten?". We said "No". He said "Come and have breakfast with me". We spent all morning with him. Sitting in the hotel, talking about tours, The Game album, Flash Gordon. That's a nice little memory of Brian.

Freddie Mercury. One of my favourite memories of Freddie was when we went to Ally Pally. Just as they were finishing the filming of the 'Save Me' video, in the afternoon, I went backstage. A friend of mine had printed some photos of the Liverpool Empire show, earlier in the month. I said to Fred "Could you sign that please?". There was one in particular that he liked. He said "That's a good photo". I said "That's one that my mate took at Liverpool Empire". Freddie said "And these are for?". I said "It's for me" and Freddie wrote "To Jim". I turned to my mate and said "Oh my God! He knows my name!". Freddie said "Of course I know your name Darling! You've been with us forever!". I nearly fell over.

Back in 1992, Queen's official biography, written by yourself and Jacky Gunn was published. It impressed me by being the first Queen book to go into the band's career in real depth, in a really intelligent, respectful way. How did that book come about?

I'd gone down to the Queen office in 1986 to pick up my passes. I was going to Zurich, Ireland and the U.K gigs (Manchester, Newcastle, Wembley and Knebworth). The band's secretary, Julie, said "I'm glad you're here now, take this home with you and read it. It's a biography that someone is writing on Queen, he'd like our involvement with it. I said "Yeah, okay I'll read it".

I started reading it on the train, going home. I'm reading it thinking, "That's rubbish!", "That's not true!"

"I know more than that! What about this? what about that?". I took it back to the office after the Magic Tour had finished and said to Julie "This is a load of rubbish".

So, she said, "Oh... okay... could you tell me why it's a load of rubbish?". I said, "I could do a better job than that!"

Julie said, "Go on then, if you think you can do a better job than that, do it". So, I did.

I spent a year planning what I wanted to do and speaking to Jacky about it. I wanted it to be all about the music, not private stuff or nonsense stories. Facts, figures and stories about the music.

My cousin worked in a binder's and she did it for me at work. I took it down to Julie and said "There you are, there are my plans, I've written keynotes". I thought 'that will get them'. I wanted them to think 'He does know his stuff' and of course it worked!

Freddie said to me (about a particular fact in the book) "How did you know that?". I said "I did my homework". He looked at me and smiled. Freddie had always said to me, "All they ever want to know is if I'm gay and why I paint my nails black. They don't do their homework". So, when I said "I did my homework", he knew exactly what I was referring to.

It took a few months and then Julie rang me up and said "You've got the green light! The band have agreed that you should write it and they will help you, all four of them. You can go to their homes and speak to them and you can go to their parents and speak to them too. Queen Productions will help you. We will have to do it officially and get contracts signed". That's how it happened. There is no other Queen book that has ever had the involvement of all four members of the band and there never can.

A few Queen fans have asked whether there will ever be an updated version?

Watch this space.

Why do you think Queen are more popular than ever?

I think they are even more popular today than they were when Freddie Mercury was alive. The songs are much stronger than even I thought they would be, they seem to touch a nerve with everybody. I think also, the diversity of the music has helped. I don't think there's a band like them, they are unique. Let's take for instance 'Don't Stop Me Now'. A song that, when they recorded it for the album, the guitarist didn't like it. He wasn't happy playing on it but the other three were like "No, this is a good song".

That song just seems to keep coming back for new generations. More importantly, young people, kids, school leaders, University people seem to grab that song as their song. If you listen to it today, it sounds just as good as it did in 1978. A forty-two-year-old song that sounds fresh today.

Also, the gigs. Freddie has gone. They brought in somebody to sing in place of him, which is a cause of controversy with a lot of the older fans. You have someone like Adam Lambert who is performing the songs with Brian and Roger. They sold 400,000 tickets in the U.K. and around the world they are selling a ridiculous amount of tickets. People want to see them. Brian, Roger and a lot of people have accepted that whoever is singing at the front, it can't be Freddie, it's impossible, he's gone. In a live situation, they are still out there and I think that is helping to keep the name of the band alive. Although it's not Queen as you and I know them, it's Queen plus whoever they have got fronting the band. Currently it's this guy, who is helping them shift a lot of tickets.

It's amazing because, as you know Jim, I am very much into my vinyl records and if you look at the vinyl community on YouTube there are lots of young people showing off their Queen collections, their Beatles collections, their Led Zeppelin collections. You'd think that these kids would only be interested in music from the current era but these classic bands have a massive popularity.

Well that, to me, speaks volumes! [laughs] For some reason, I think the music of those bands you just mentioned is going to be around forever. In the truest sense of the word, forever. When you and I have both gone, this article might get found in one hundred years' time and someone will read it and say "Ooh I'll read this and I might stick some albums on". Who are they going to be playing? Led Zeppelin. The Beatles. Queen. I don't think it will be anyone from 2020 and that speaks volumes. For some reason, bands from the '60s, '70s and '80s are going to be around forever, especially bands like those three. When you think about it, it's quite incredible.

Jim Jenkins was speaking with David Geldard

*Originally published in **We Are Cult**, 11 May 2020.*

Funny How Love Is

David Geldard

Perhaps the most difficult part of putting this book together is articulating what Queen mean to me. I am not sure that mere words can do that. They have been a soundtrack to my life, they have made the good times even better and given me strength when things were bad. Their music has so many memories involving loved ones no longer here. It's bizarre that as I sit here writing this, so many cherished friendships I have were formed over our mutual love of Queen come to mind. I can't imagine what my life would have been like without them, these four guys that I have never even met.

To explain, I think we need to go way back to the beginning. In 1973, the top grossing film was the supernatural horror movie 'The Exorcist'. The most watched TV event was the wedding of Princess Anne to Mark Philips and, on 13 July, a certain band called Queen released their self-titled debut album. In the Christmas of that year, I decided to vacate my Mum's womb where I had been kindly living, rent free, for the past 9 months whilst all this was going on.

We lived in a terraced house in Edgeley, Stockport. In fact it was literally on the doorstep of Stockport County F.C.'s ground, Edgeley Park. My parents were quite young, already married but only 19 years old at the time of my birth. As such, music was a big deal in our house.

In the 1970s, there were only three TV channels in the UK: BBC 1, BBC 2 and ITV. Even those broadcast only intermittently in the daytime. Therefore, it seems that everyone listened to the radio a lot more.

It's weird, but as a kid, your main focus isn't rock and pop music. You are playing, drawing, maybe just watching TV. Music is an incredible force though. It can secretly worm itself into your brain when you think you weren't even paying attention, but years later you can hear a piece of music and it transports you back to that time and place.

My Mum and Dad's record collection was mainly made up of The Beatles, Motown (particularly Stevie Wonder), E.L.O., Gilbert O' Sullivan and Queen.

When people ask me if I can remember the first time I heard Queen, I can't. It's like asking me when I first heard 'Happy Birthday'. For me, they have always been there. I recalled this to my Mum recently and she told me, "I can remember when you first heard Queen. You were sat in the back of your Grandad's car with me and 'Killer Queen' came on the radio, during Radio One's Top 40 show".

My earliest Queen memory I have is 'Bohemian Rhapsody'. My Dad bought the single and it was played over and over in our house. The video stuck in my mind, as I am sure it was played on TV for many years after it left the charts. To this day, it's my favourite song of all time, I never get tired of it. In many ways, it's such an obvious choice that perhaps I should lie and say it's 'Tenement Funster' or 'Ogre Battle', to show off my 'true Queen fan' credentials. But honestly, if you were to measure the serotonin in my head, I'm sure it would go off the scale whenever I hear 'Bohemian Rhapsody'.

Every Thursday night at our house, the TV was tuned into 'Top Of The Pops', which in those days was the only way to see music videos in the UK.

It's funny when I think back to my childhood first impressions of bands I now love. Rock stars didn't look like members of your family or the people you saw shopping when you were out with your parents. They seemed a little odd. Pink Floyd's 'Another Brick In The Wall' video disturbed me as a kid, as did David Bowie's 'Ashes to Ashes' when I saw it on 'Top Of The Pops'. At that age, you aren't understanding it's just an act. My first impressions of Queen are quite amusing now. To my infant mind, Queen were probably yobbos who liked getting drunk, smashing things up and making a proper racket. That lead singer, Freddie, he's so obviously obsessed with girls that have big bottoms.

When I eventually heard the members of Queen speak on telly for the first time, I was absolutely shocked. Especially Freddie, he sounded so posh! Brian, Roger and John sounded so intelligent, calm and normal.

The next big Queen milestone for me was 'Flash Gordon'. As a kid who was utterly obsessed with 'Doctor Who' and 'Star Wars', this was a big deal to me. It was a while before I saw the film but I'd seen the cartoons and the Buster Crabbe serial. When I listened to the 'Flash' single, I used to create images in my mind of what I thought was happening in the film.

Christmas 1981 and my Dad received Queen's 'Greatest Hits' on vinyl, from my Mum. That record got played over and over for so many years. I'm surprised the vinyl didn't turn transparent. Looking back, my parents were very kind to me and never minded me using the family stereo or playing their records. The two I would always go for was Queen's 'Greatest Hits' and The Beatles' 'Blue Album'. I would sit for hours listening to those two albums on my parents' headphones.

As I got to my final year in primary school – 1984/85 – my interest in music increased. I had two older cousins who were into Duran Duran, Depeche Mode, Wham! and so on. They used to bring round their ghetto blaster to our house, along with the latest issue of 'Smash Hits' magazine.

I started listening to a slightly wider range of music but Queen were still a favourite and 'Top Of The Pops' was still unmissable. I recall the first time 'Radio Ga Ga' aired on the programme. My Dad wasn't taken with it at all at first. He thought they had strayed too far from the Queen sound. It wasn't long before it came to be one of his best-loved Queen songs.

I was totally shocked when I found out that the video for 'I Want to Break Free' caused such outrage in the USA. I can distinctly remember seeing it for the first time as a family and we all laughed our heads off. Being Mancunians, it was more than obvious that this was a pastiche of 'Coronation Street'. Also, entertainers dressing in drag was nothing new to the British, it's an age old tradition going back to the days of music hall. I'd grown up seeing all my favourite comedians dressed as women, 'Monty Python', 'The Two Ronnies' and of course, Freddie's mate Kenny Everett (who was very much loved in our house). The whole idea that it created such uproar across the pond was bizarre to most of us in the UK, we never batted an eyelid.

December 1984 and we were called into a special assembly at my primary school, Banks Lane Junior School. We entered the assembly hall to hear the sound of the new charity record 'Do They Know It's Christmas?' by Band Aid. It featured most of the bands that my school mates were into. Everyone was talking about it. The images of Ethiopian famine, broadcast on BBC News, were heartbreaking. This was a big deal. The headmaster informed us of the situation and the background to the record. It was the first time ever that pop music had entered the discussion in a school assembly. This was a serious, huge event.

I can remember having a discussion in a cookery lesson, with a fellow Queen-loving mate, Neil Jefferies, whilst making mince pies. "I wonder why Queen aren't on the Band Aid record?". The teacher interjected "Perhaps they were on tour or something?".

A few months passed and after the record-breaking success of the Band Aid single, Live Aid was announced. This time Queen were involved. Everyone in the playground was talking about it. Who was going to be the best band? I always got the impression, at the time, that most of my schoolmates liked Queen but they weren't seen as 'trendy'. All the talk was of Duran Duran, Spandau Ballet, Ultravox. The 'Smash Hits' crowd.

Saturday 13 July 1985. We had just moved house that week. We sat, as a family, in front of the TV for Live Aid. From memory, it was a boiling hot day. As the show kicked in with Status Quo and I saw the audience reaction, I turned to my Mum and said, "I wish I was there!".

I watched all the artists and enjoyed all of them to various degrees. It was something of an education in music. Further on in the afternoon, the energy seemed to dip a bit. Phil Collins, Sting, Howard Jones, Bryan Ferry and Sade all performed slow ballads. They were good enough but something was just missing. Live Aid did much to help propel U2 to mega-stardom as their brilliant set was much talked about afterwards. Dire Straits were riding high on the success of 'Brothers In Arms' at Live Aid. Whilst their performance was good, it lacked a certain something.

As soon as Smith And Jones introduced Queen, it was blindingly obvious how much the crowd loved the band. Freddie came onstage smiling and just looked 'up for it'. I don't know whether or not he was nervous but he gave the impression that he wanted to really enjoy himself. That was sensed by the crowd and reciprocated, I think. There's a lot that has been said about Freddie and Queen on that day, but ultimately they shone brighter than the whole cast of rock and roll legends at Live Aid. I think you have to credit them for having the intelligence to understand exactly what was needed and how to make the best impression. The big hits, no messing about. They put in the necessary preparation and they were a finely tuned machine by that point anyway. They had just played Rock in Rio to 250,000 a few months earlier. The band were so professional. I suppose there is always a certain amount of luck in any performance but even though I have watched that set a million times, it still makes me grin from ear to ear. Brian, Roger and John played perfectly. Freddie sang his heart out and was on great form, but a lot of it, for me, was the way Freddie projected himself. He didn't come on with the usual rock star attitude of not smiling and trying to be cool. He was full of energy and joy, the audience sensed it and were with him every step of the way.

When you have been stood up all day at an outdoor gig or festival in the heat, you need upbeat music and something that you can participate in. Queen were absolutely what that event needed.

I watched as much of the rest of Live Aid as I could. David Bowie was brilliant. Poor Paul McCartney suffered a faulty microphone and couldn't be heard. Let's face it though, that day belonged to Queen.

From this moment on, I didn't just like Queen, I was a proper fan. Luckily, although times were tough for Northern working class families in the mid 1980s, my Uncle Alan owned every album on vinyl. He kindly lent them to me and I taped them all. (Dear Brian, Roger and John, I am sorry but I did later buy all the albums myself, several times over!).

When faced with the entire Queen catalogue, 'A Night at the Opera' was the one that initially stood out for me. It sounded like a hard rock 'Sgt. Pepper'. So many different styles and detours. Music hall, heavy metal, space-folk, ballads... it had everything. All those albums got played so much and I was word perfect within a short space of time.

In June 1986, Queen released the album 'A Kind of Magic'. Luckily for me, my maternal Grandad had just given me £10, so I ran down to Our Price in Stockport straight away to buy it. This was my first experience of buying an album.

That Summer, Queen were playing live in the UK on The Magic Tour. I asked my parents if we could go to the show at Manchester City's ground, Maine Road. To this day, I am not sure why we didn't. It could have been that my Mum was anxious about me going to an open air rock concert at a young age. It could have been that it sold out. Another reason may have been that we were a working-class family, I had two younger brothers and times were quite difficult in the mid 1980s. My Dad said, "I will take you next time".

There was some consolation though. In October 1986, Channel 4's ground-breaking music show 'The Tube', showed 'Real Magic'. This was a 90 minute version of the 1986 Wembley gig (which later became known as 'Queen – Live at Wembley'). Before stereo TV arrived in the UK this was broadcast as a 'simulcast'. The stereo sound was broadcast simultaneously on Independent Local Radio. It would be a few months later when we got our first video cassette recorder, but I recorded the audio, which lasted me until the official release came out.

I could not get over how great this concert was, I had never seen a concert on TV like it. It was perfection. I wanted to be a musician. In fact, I wanted to be Brian May! This inspired me to buy a secondhand guitar from my school mate, Daniel Collier. I set about having guitar lessons at school, which were ditched after about five weeks of getting bored silly of tapping on the back of it to 'She'll Be Coming Round the Mountain When She Comes'. I wasn't going to become Brian May by doing this nonsense. I set about teaching myself by reading books and playing by ear. I never did become another Dr. May, but I was in band in my twenties and I found out what it was like to record an album and play loads of gigs. Another of my mates from school, Stephen Eason, was equally obsessed with Queen and Brian May. He has now gone on to make several of his own guitars, inspired by Brian.

A couple of years later, I was walking across our local recreation ground when I saw one of my old Primary School pals, Jon Fowler, sat on a fence talking to a mate. He shouted to me, "Hey Dave, who do you reckon is better, Queen or Michael Jackson?"

I replied, "Queen, of course."

We hadn't spoken for a few years, but I had discovered that he had become a massive Queen fan. We started chatting about what stuff we did and didn't own and then started swapping videos and albums.

We became close due to our love of Queen. We would go round to each other's teenage bedrooms and blast our favourite albums and update each other on our latest purchases. One day, Jon said to me "Have you seen this? I've got a bootleg of Queen at Maine Road!"

I'd read about bootlegs but never encountered one before. Even though the sound was quite poor when compared to a regular album, there was something quite exciting about getting to listen to something which hadn't been released and most people didn't own.

This collecting of the band's material led us down so many other musical rabbit holes. The Cross, Smile, Peter Straker, Ian Hunter, Billy Squier, Eddie Howell, these were artists who were not troubling the higher reaches of the charts, but we became really into them whilst the rest of the world was digging Kylie and Jason and Bros.

Even the bands that had supported Queen or were good mates with them became favourites. David Bowie, Def Leppard, Big Country, Status Quo, Thin Lizzy, Mott the Hoople and so on.

In 1989, Queen released 'The Miracle'. Jon and I had gotten quite into heavy rock and had ditched the likes of 'Smash Hits' magazine in favour of 'Kerrang!' and 'Q' magazine. We were utterly delighted when the first single released from the album was the guitar heavy 'I Want it All'. The masters were back!

1989 was a particularly hot summer and I recall driving around Manchester with my Grandad in his Ford Granada, in the hot sun with 'Breakthru' blaring on the radio and the window down. I was 15 at the time and my youngest brother, Nicholas was 4 years old. When we put 'Breakthru' on at home, we would both grab a pair of Nick's toy tennis rackets and play air guitar. He liked to pretend we were Queen playing on The Miracle Express train.

As much as everybody was loving 'The Miracle' album, something seemed wrong. Freddie had publicly said that he didn't want to tour. This didn't seem like Freddie or Queen. They seemed to be pioneers of stadium rock touring. No band ever looked as though they were having as much fun on stage as Queen.

It was around this time that people started to comment on Freddie's appearance and rumours started. HIV/AIDS was all over the TV and press in those days. There was the chilling public information film voiced by actor John Hurt, which was enough to scare anyone away from a sexual relationship.

There were educational TV programmes telling you to limit your partners and showing you how to put on a condom. The British tabloid press being what it is was also quite homophobic at the time, blaming the gay community for the disease.

There were plenty of rumours about Freddie and the decision not to tour 'The Miracle' album made many of us worry. When Queen appeared at the BRIT awards in 1990, Freddie's appearance worried us even more. He looked like he had lost a lot of weight.

31 December 1990. My parents had gone shopping to get some supplies for New Year's Eve. I was sitting in the house listening to BBC Radio One, the Simon Bates show. He said, "Next up, we've got the new single from Queen, 'Innuendo'." When he played it, my jaw hit the floor. I couldn't believe how fantastic it was. That Christmas I had received Led Zeppelin's 'Remasters' album on CD from my Mum and Dad. 'Innuendo' sounded like Fred

Zep! A long epic that recalled, in parts, 'Queen II', 'Bohemian Rhapsody', and Zeppelin's 'Kashmir'. I was buzzing.

A few weeks later, 'Innuendo' was riding high in the UK charts at number one. This felt like vindication of how great Queen still were. I was at college at this time and Manchester was now the coolest city on Earth due to bands like The Stone Roses, The Happy Mondays, The Inspiral Carpets and James. Most people at college adopted the fashion and dressed in flared jeans and James T-Shirts. I quite liked some of the singles but I wasn't really bothered about those bands. Queen's 'Innuendo' was the soundtrack to my 1991. I also started working a part time job at Superdrug in Stockport. This meant that I could afford to add to my CD collection every week!

On Saturday 23 November 1991, Freddie issued a press release stating that he had AIDS. It was heartbreaking, but a lot of us had suspected that this was the case for a while. At the back of my mind, I naively thought, "But he's Freddie Mercury, he will be able to afford the best healthcare and the best Doctors, maybe he will be around for a few more years yet and they'll find a cure?".

As we know, Freddie died the next night at his home, Garden Lodge in Kensington, London.

On the morning of Monday 25 November, as I lay sleeping in bed, my Dad knocked on my bedroom door. "David. Freddie Mercury has died". I couldn't believe it. I was absolutely gutted. I switched the radio on in my room and 'We Are the Champions' was playing on Radio One. I went downstairs and TV-am (one of the two UK breakfast options at the time) was reporting on the loss of Freddie. Fans were already outside Garden Lodge, laying flowers and in tears.

I didn't want to go into college that day. My Mum encouraged me to. Everyone was talking about it and there were a fair few homophobic idiots making vile comments. I remember a teacher standing with students in the corridor and putting some of them right. He seemed an unlikely 'gay ally', a proper beer drinking, pub dwelling 'blokey bloke', but I remember him telling the students that his favourite singer, Johnny Mathis, was also gay. Freddie's death was also a wake-up call for a lot of people. Rock Hudson had died from the disease, but he wasn't really that well known or popular with my generation. Everybody knew who Freddie was. This was easily the biggest rock star death since John Lennon.

I went to my part time job that evening. In those days, Stockport was a busy shopping town. Every single shop was blaring out Queen that night.

'Bohemian Rhapsody' was re-released that Christmas and went straight to number one again. You couldn't go to any pub, party or family gathering that Christmas without hearing a load of Queen songs. It seemed like the whole country was mourning but also celebrating the life of Freddie Mercury.

In early 1992, Brian and Roger announced The Freddie Mercury Tribute Concert at the BRIT Awards. I was jumping around the living room in a panic. There was absolutely no way I was going to miss out on this. The next day, it had sold out.

This wasn't going to stop me. I remembered that a local independent record shop, Music Zone, did coach inclusive concert packages. By chance, I rang them to see if they had bought them for the Freddie gig.

Luckily, they had been allocated six tickets! My Mum had decided that I wasn't to miss college, so she would go and queue up first thing in the morning. Heroically, she managed to get four of the six tickets.

On the morning of 20 April 1992, Easter Monday, my Dad, my mate Jon, my cousin Steve and myself boarded a coach outside the Garrick Theatre in Stockport and headed off with a bunch of Queen fans to Wembley. The driver played a bootleg tape of Queen's Elland Road (Leeds) gig from 1982 on a loop all the way down there. Everyone on the bus was talking about which acts were going to appear. It read like a 'Who's Who' of my own record collection. Def Leppard, David Bowie, Robert Plant, Guns N' Roses, Extreme, Metallica, Roger Daltrey, Tony Iommi, Mick Ronson, Ian Hunter, Elton John and even though they weren't in the stadium, a video appearance by U2.

As we arrived outside Wembley, there were thousands of people in front of us, queueing up those famous steps. The T-shirts had already completely sold out. The guy who dressed as Freddie who appeared on much of the TV footage was in the same queue as us. As soon as he got to the top of the steps, he turned around and started singing 'Radio Ga Ga'. All the fans clapped along, even the police on horseback couldn't resist joining in the fun. Then a Scouser made everyone laugh by shouting "At least Freddie could sing, like!".

I also walked past Queen Fan Club president Jacky Smith, who I recognised off the 'Magic Years' video, but I was too shy to say hello.

Once in the stadium, we walked straight near the front. The first half was incredible. The concert opened with an emotional intro from Brian May, Roger Taylor and John Deacon. Deaky then introduced the opening act , Metallica! The American thrash quartet may not have seemed like an obvious choice to open the concert, but they had just hit the big time with 'The Black Album' and enough of the audience seemed to enjoy the mega hit 'Enter Sandman'.

I was lapping up every minute, I'd been a Metallica fan since a school friend lent me 'Master of Puppets'. Next up onstage were Boston funk-metallers Extreme, who played a blinder by opting to do a Queen medley. As soon as Gary Cherone started singing the intro to 'Mustapha', Extreme had Queen's audience eating out of the palms of their hands.

Following Extreme, legendary Sheffield rockers Def Leppard hit the stage. This was a huge thrill for me, as I had been a mega fan since I saw them perform 'Animal' on 'Top Of The Pops' back in 1987. This was Leppard's first major appearance since the tragic death of guitarist Steve Clark back in 1991 and the first major performance featuring new guitar player Vivian Campell. Leppard blasted into 'Animal' before performing their latest hit at the time, 'Let's Get Rocked'. The highlight, however, was when their long-time friend, Brian

May, joined them onstage for a rip-roaring version of the 'Sheer Heart Attack' classic, 'Now I'm Here'.

Bob Geldof came onstage and performed an acoustic number, 'Too Late God' before introducing the legendary Spinal Tap, who added some humour to proceedings, something, which Freddie would surely have approved of.

On the video screens, Cindy Crawford introduced specially shot live footage of U2 from a gig in Sacremento, California. Next it was the turn of the controversial Guns N' Roses. Many wondered if they would even show up, such was their reputation at the time. They needed have worried. At this point, Guns N' Roses were arguably the biggest band in the world and in the footage, you can see that reflected in the audience's reaction to them. They performed a storming version of 'Paradise City' which ended with über-Queen fan Axl Rose shouting, "England! Long live Freddie!". They performed a verse of Alice Cooper's 'Only Women Bleed' before going into their version of Bob Dylan's 'Knocking on Heaven's Door', which included some fantastic audience participation. Guns N' Roses looked genuinely pleased to be participating and there was no doubting their credentials as Queen and Freddie fans.

Something that gets lost when the concert is repeated on TV is that on the day, in between the changeover of the acts, lots of footage of Freddie and Queen music videos were shown on the big screen. That was as integral as any of the bands. It really felt as though Freddie was there in a way. There was so much singing along, clapping, laughing, and crying in the audience. It was a day of so many emotions.

In the days when Freddie was ill, he suffered from so much press intrusion and unkind things said in the British tabloid papers. This almost felt like 70,000 of Freddie's biggest allies, including the cream of the music world, turning around, and saying to those critics, "Fuck you! We think he was brilliant!".

The second half of the show featured the remaining three members of Queen with guest vocalists, but just before they hit the stage, Ian McKellan appeared on the video screens and introduced Elizabeth Taylor to the Wembley stage. Elizabeth Taylor paid tribute to Freddie in her speech and addressed the AIDS crisis. She also expertly dealt with a heckler, much to the delight of the Wembley crowd. There is something quite surreal about seeing someone that famous in front of you.

Freddie appeared on the screens performing his famous 'Day-Oh!' from Live Aid. The pyros went off and May, Taylor and Deacon hit the stage performing 'Tie Your Mother Down'. For the first time I was seeing the members of Queen together in real life after being such a huge fan for years. I was trying to process it because in that moment, being in the crowd, was so exciting. Then, Joe Elliott (my favourite vocalist after Freddie) joined them on the song. If that wasn't enough, guitar god Slash then joined in. My excitement levels were through the roof. One just wished that Freddie was up there with them.

Following short intros of Black Sabbath's 'Heaven and Hell' and The Who's 'Pinball Wizard', Daltrey and Iommi joined Queen for a powerful run through 'I Want It All'. A song which, sadly, Queen never got to perform live. Then followed Italian vocalist Zucchero for a passionate performance of the underrated 'Hot Space' song, 'Las Palabras D'Amour'.

Tony Iommi re-joined Queen onstage and they were, in turn, joined by Extreme's Gary Cherone for 'Hammer to Fall' and Metallica's James Hetfield for 'Stone Cold Crazy' (Metallica's cover of the song had been the B-side to 'Enter Sandman').

Led Zeppelin legend – and hero to Freddie – Robert Plant took to the stage. Queen and Plant launched into the track 'Innuendo'. In my own personal view, Robert Plant has been unduly harsh on his own performance of this song. He forgot a couple of words and his voice struggled a little, but all in all, I think it was a great performance of a masterpiece of a song from the final album released during Freddie's lifetime. It wasn't perfect, but that is live music for you. After a brief verse of Led Zeppelin's 'Thank You', Plant and Queen delivered an awesome version of 'Crazy Little Thing Called Love'.

It was then time for Brian May to perform a previously unheard song 'Too Much Love Will Kill You', which would appear on his solo album 'Back to the Light' and on the posthumous Queen album, 'Made in Heaven'. It was a heartfelt version of the song and considering the circumstances, it can't have been easy for him to perform. The audience was with him all the way.

It was then time for some of the more pop-orientated performers to take the stage. Paul Young led the crowd through 'Radio Ga Ga'. Seal, who was one of the U.K.'s biggest stars at this point, gave his vocal weight to 'Who Wants to Live Forever'.

Lisa Stansfield appeared in Hilda Ogden-style curlers with a vacuum cleaner and performed 'I Want to Break Free'. In doing so she perfectly paid tribute to Freddie's camp humour.

Things really moved up a gear when Roger Taylor introduced David Bowie and Annie Lennox to sing Queen and Bowie's 1981 number one smash 'Under Pressure'. Bowie looked suave in his lime green suit and Annie Lennox looked as though her outfit had been inspired by Darryl Hannah in 'Blade Runner'.

One of the most emotional moments of the night, for me anyway, came next. Bowie and Queen were joined by Mott the Hoople's Ian Hunter, The Spiders From Mars' (and Hunter's sideman since 1974) Mick Ronson alongside Def Leppard's Joe Elliott and Phil Collen for a powerhouse performance of 'All the Young Dudes', the song Bowie had written for Mott twenty years earlier just as the band were on the verge of splitting up. This was a highly significant moment, as Queen got their big break supporting Mott the Hoople back in 1973. In the stadium, the video screens zoomed in to Joe Elliott's face. A huge fan of Mott, Bowie and Queen, I thought "How is HE feeling right now?". It was a real highlight, an incredible moment.

Bowie and Ronson then launched into 'Heroes'. This performance has extra resonance now, as it was Mick Ronson's last [Ronson died of liver cancer the following April, aged 46]. Bowie dropped to one knee at the end and delivered the Lord's

Prayer. It was a move that has since been mocked and criticised, but I think it was done with the best of intentions. By this stage, these performers had lost a lot of friends to this dreadful disease.

At the time, my friends and I considered George Michael to be more of a lightweight 'pop' artist. So, for him to come on and do ''39', a deep cut from 'A Night at the Opera', was quite the surprise.

George performed a duet with Lisa Stansfield on 'These are the Days of Our Lives'. Those of us who were there will forever remember the tears in the audience.

Then came the show's most iconic moment. George Michael performing 'Somebody to Love'. There was mutual admiration between Freddie Mercury and George Michael and Freddie himself surely would have been proud of this moment.

The recording of this performance was to reach number one in the UK Singles chart the following year.

Elton John took to the piano, unannounced, and launched into Queen's magnum opus 'Bohemian Rhapsody'. This was one of the most emotional moments of my life. Being stood in a stadium with 72,000 other fans singing 'Bo Rhap' at the top of their voices, just five months after Freddie Mercury's death, gives me goosebumps now just thinking about it. As the song morphed into its heavy metal section, Axl Rose took to the stage like a Tasmanian Devil, in an American Football shirt, a kilt and boots. The crowd went wild. As Axl and Elton finish the song (apparently all unrehearsed) you can see the delight on Roger Taylor's face.

Elton continued with 'The Show Must Go On', followed by Axl Rose's powerful take on 'We Will Rock You'.

It was only fitting that another of Freddie's biggest heroes closed the show – Liza Minelli. Liza was joined by the rest of the performers for a rendition of 'We are the Champions'. Freddie was surely looking down smiling.

As well left the stadium, under the video screen of the left side of the stage, we got a cheery wave from Spinal Tap as they got into their limo. It was a surreal but lovely moment ending a superb but emotional day.

I was 18 years old at the time of the concert. Less than 24 hours later after being a few feet away from Queen performing with all these legends, I was back at my part time college job at Superdrug in Stockport, stacking cans of Panda pop. It seemed like it had been a dream. It took me a long time to come down from that day and it remains my favourite concert that I have ever been to.

It was also around this time that 'tribute nights' seemed to start up. Whenever there was a Queen Tribute Night in our area, we would go. At this time, they weren't really the type of tribute night that happens now. They consisted mainly of discos that played Queen records, maybe with video screens too. These happened at long-gone venues such as The Acton Court and Quaffers in Stockport, Squires pub in Didsbury and many more. One of the first tribute bands we used to follow was called 'Magic – A Kind of Queen'. They looked absolutely nothing like the band but sounded pretty good. It was also a great opportunity to meet other Queen fans.

By far, the best Queen tribute nights were put on in Horwich, near Bolton by Denise Horwich, who features in this book.

In the Autumn of 1992, Brian May released his solo album 'Back To The Light'. It was followed the next year by a tour. My Dad, my mate Jon, Lisa (his then girlfriend) and myself went to see The Brian May Band at the Manchester Apollo on 8 June 1993. It was a hot, sweaty night and the legendary Apollo was packed out. It was so exciting, not least because for many years, Brian had not played at a venue of this size. Of course, we had never seen him perform solo before either. We were all big lovers of Brian May's solo material. Brian had assembled a truly amazing group of musicians including Spike Edney, Jamie Moses, Neil Murray, Catherine Porter, Shelley Preston and the legendary Cozy Powell.

In the days before setlists getting posted all over the internet, it was truly a surprise and a thrill when every number was performed. I miss that. I remember Brian playing such much loved Queen classics as 'Now I'm Here', 'Tie Your Mother Down' and a particularly moving rendition of 'Love Of My Life', which kind of takes on its own life when the band and the audience become one. I can still remember that moment as if it was yesterday. It was one of my Dad's favourite songs and it was priceless to see him enjoy it so much. My Dad passed in 2003 at the very young age of 49 and these memories mean everything to me. Another great memory from this gig was just how good Cozy Powell was. Watching him, hearing him and feeling those drums reverberate through your body was quite the experience.

I admired both Brian and Roger so much for performing solo after Freddie died. It was brave and a lot of these songs had so much emotional significance to them.

The following year, Roger Taylor released his third solo album (not including those by The Cross). This was entitled 'Happiness?'. It's a fantastic album which manages at times to recall both John Lennon and Pink Floyd. Roger's vocals are nicely complimented by Jason Falloon's Gimour-esque guitars.

Roger toured this album and on 3 December, Jon Fowler, myself and another friend saw him play live at Manchester University debating halls. We did make a failed attempt to try to meet Roger backstage before the gig. In all honesty, I think it was me that got cold feet. These guys are such huge heroes to me, I'd probably freeze if I met them.

At this gig we were probably about three feet away in front of Roger. He came on to 'A Kind of Magic' and performed many songs from 'Happiness?', as well as many well-known Queen classics. The absolute highlight for me was when he sang 'Tenement Funster' from 'Sheer Heart Attack'. The whole audience knew every word and I had never heard this song sung anywhere other than on the original album. It was magical. I recall he also did great covers of The Beatles' 'Twist and Shout' and the Jimi Hendrix classic 'Voodoo Chile'. An unforgettable gig.

On 6 November 1995, Queen released the posthumous album 'Made in Heaven', featuring Freddie's final work. It was a remarkable record and one I loved straight away. There was such a mix of emotions though. Some fantastic new songs but considering the context in which they were made, it made listening to it a very touching experience.

I played it solidly, every day for a month, until 7 December 1995. The worst day of my life. My youngest brother, Nicholas, died of a brain haemorrhage, caused by an aneurysm. He was aged ten.

There is no way I can convey this experience in mere words. It was life-changing and altered the person I am. You lose a certain innocence about life when you experience something like that. I was still living at home, with my parents and my other brother Christopher at the time. All of us were heartbroken beyond words.

Nick loved life. He loved football, he loved video games, he loved music. Particularly Queen. He'd been brought up listening to them. He had recently been on a weekend trip to London with my Mum and Dad and had brought me back a Freddie Mercury mug, something which I still have and treasure. A few days after his death, his Christmas present to me came through the post. It was a Queen book.

I am not going to lie, I struggled to get over his death, we all did. Everyone deals with these events differently but listening to music always helped me to cope. I struggled to listen to 'Made In Heaven' for a long time after that because of its connection to that last day I saw Nick. There's not a day that goes by that I don't miss him.

Roger and Brian both toured again in the late 1990s and I attended both gigs with my old mate Jon Fowler. Both gigs were, again, incredible and this time both my Mum and Dad came to see Brian. I always remember a group of lads who called themselves 'The John Deacon Fan Club' who attended both those gigs. They dressed from head to toe like John Deacon on the Magic Tour, complete with curly wigs and tight 1980s shorts.

After the Roger Taylor gig in 1999 at Manchester University, we piled into the bar with these lads and it soon turned into an alcohol fuelled sing along, with the Deaky fan club all playing air bass. One song segued into another and before long the whole bar was filled with Queen fans singing loudly. When it got to 'Love Of My Life', we were so loud that the bar staff had had enough. We were asked to leave. It was all good-natured fun; we were just high on seeing Roger live.

In 2003, I met my wife, Carol. The love of my life. Strangely, although she respects their musical ability, she is not a Queen fan. Carol is older than me and her youth was spent enjoying the post-punk scene and bands like The Smiths, The Cure and Blondie. Carol has always been supportive of my Queen obsession though, and for my Christmas and birthday presents she always seeks out cool Queen stuff. Considering Queen are not her favourite band, she never complains about me playing them at full blast all the time.

In the mid 2000s, Queen toured with Paul Rodgers. I attended both the tours and although this pairing

Editor David Geldard with Queen's official biographer Jim Jenkins at charity event 'A BowieMian Rhapsody' in aid of the Royal Manchester Children's Hospital. [Photo © D. Geldard]

might have been Marmite to some, I absolutely adored it. My love of Free and Bad Company went back to 1991, when Free had re-released 'Alright Now' on the back of a successful commercial for Wrigley's Chewing Gum. I bought their 'Best Of's' within the first few months of working and Queen playing with Paul Rodgers seemed like an ideal match to me.

I get why some people weren't into it. Music is a very personal thing and it's very difficult when you have someone fronting Queen who isn't Freddie Mercury. No one can replace him, but it was a great experience for those who wanted to go out and hear those songs performed live.

In recent years, thanks to the internet bringing people closer together, I have become good friends with some of the people who have contributed to this book. I became good friends with Jim Jenkins when we organised a fundraising Queen-themed event for the Royal Manchester Children's Hospital back in 2019.

A couple of years later, I got my own Classic Rock radio show on Manchester's FAB Radio International and whilst DJing a second fundraising event with Jim, he asked me if I fancied DJing at the Fan Club Convention. How could I resist?

It was such a great experience and an absolute honour. I met so many great Queen fans and it was such a buzz to hear people cheer when you played their favourite Queen songs. At the convention, it's often not the most obvious ones that are the most popular. Roger's 'Man On Fire' and Brian's 'Star Fleet' are absolute floor fillers! I just couldn't work out why it had taken me so long to go to the Convention, it was one of the most enjoyable experiences of my life.

As I said at the beginning, I can't quite put into words what Queen and their music mean to me. They have truly been a soundtrack to my life. I have many friends who I would never have met if it hadn't been for Queen. I probably would have never picked up a guitar or been a DJ too if it hadn't been for them.

Their music has been there for me through the bad times and the good.

I look forward to many more years of listening to their music and sharing good times with people. Because that's what life is all about. Love, people and music.

ARTWORK © JIM SANGSTER

Very Special Thanks

David would like to thank:

My wife **Carol Barker**, for unwavering support and encouragement. I couldn't have done this without you. You are the best!

My parents, **David and Catherine Geldard** for a fantastic childhood and introducing me to such great music.

Jon Fowler, for friendship since childhood and sharing the love of this fantastic band. All the gigs man! The gigs!

Jim Jenkins, the encyclopedia of Queen! For encouragement, friendship and support.

Jay Gent, for coming up with the idea for this book in the first place and asking me to do it.

Special Thanks:

Andy Bacon, Linda Badder, Paul Badder, Margaret Barker, Edu Beltran, Andy Betts, Marcia Blyton, Doug Bogie, Ray Burdis, Sarah Coles, Daniel Collier, Mick Connelly, Paul Cooke , Zoe Davies, Hannah Dennis, Fontini Drakou, Cheryl Duke, Susyn Duris Elis, Shirley Dyson, Stephen Eason, FAB Radio International, Peter Freestone, Christopher Geldard, Maisie Geldard , Nicola Geldard, Oliver Geldard,

Scott Hilton, Mick Hoole, Eddie Howell, Charlotte Johnston, Chris Lee, Joe McGlynn, The Mercury Phoenix Trust , Dave Moody, Paul Moody , Clayton Moss, Paul Mount, The Official International Queen Fan Club and the Conventioneers! , Martin Padley, Pearl Padley, Amber Page, Alan G. Parker., Fiona Pass, Carl Potter, Karen Ramage, Al Rea, Paul Ripley, Gary Rothwell,Charlie Royce, Jordan M Royce, Jim Sangster, Jeff Scott Soto, Ken Shinn, Denise Silcock, Lisa Simms, Jacky Smith, Starburst Magazine, Tim Staffell , Peter Straker, Kari Van Der Beek, Paul Webb.

A big thanks to all those who have supported this book and those have contributed to this book, free of charge to raise money for The Mercury Phoenix Trust - You are the Champions!

Queen:
John Deacon, Brian May, Freddie Mercury, Roger Taylor - Thank you for the music and all the joy it has given fans around the world.

This book is dedicated to the memory of David Geldard Snr, Nicholas Geldard, Jane Geldard, Dr. John Barker and of course, Mr. Freddie Mercury.

Candy (Jay) would like to thank:

David for all the hard work, Jim for his amazing artwork, RJG for the additional proofing and editing, and all of our esteemed contributors for their memories and incredible patience. Sorry it took so long!

ALSO AVAILABLE FROM CULT INK:

A celebration of the life of one of the 20th century's true and enduring icons, *Me And The Starman* is available to buy from Amazon.

ALL PROCEEDS GO TO CANCER RESEARCH

ISBN: 9798664990546

Printed in Great Britain
by Amazon